International and Cultural Psychology

Series editor

Anthony J. Marsella, Alpharetta, GA, USA

Explores problems and challenges to mental health, psychosocial wellbeing, human growth and development, and human welfare that are emerging from our contemporary global context. It advances in psychological knowledge regarding the nature and consequences of the many social, cultural, economic, political, and environmental events and forces that affect individuals and communities throughout the world.

The series covers areas like therapy, assessment, organizational psychology, community psychology, gender, child development, and specific disorders. In addition, it addresses major global challenges such as poverty, peace, urbanization, modernization, refugees, and migration. The series acknowledges the multidisciplinary, multisectoral, and multicultural nature of the global context of our lives, and publishes books that reflect this reality.

Publish your next book in this series! Send your manuscript to Series Editor: Anthony J. Marsella, marsella@hawaii.edu.

More information about this series at http://www.springer.com/series/6089

Michael B. Salzman

A Psychology of Culture

Springer

Michael B. Salzman
Department of Educational Psychology
University of Hawai'i at Manoa
Honolulu, HI, USA

ISSN 1574-0455 ISSN 2197-7984 (electronic)
International and Cultural Psychology
ISBN 978-3-319-69418-4 ISBN 978-3-319-69420-7 (eBook)
https://doi.org/10.1007/978-3-319-69420-7

Library of Congress Control Number: 2017960417

Printed on acid-free paper

This Springer imprint is published by Springer Nature
The registered company is Springer International Publishing AG
The registered company address is: Gewerbestrasse 11, 6330 Cham, Switzerland

Preface

"Culture" has become a central focus of study across virtually all disciplines in the social sciences. The importance of culture as a mediating and/or moderating variable in education, psychology, human relations, business, and virtually all human experience has been acknowledged. This book is designed to present a specific view of culture, its psychological functions and implications for human development, and intercultural relations and adaptation. *A Psychology of Culture* could serve as a primary source for a graduate course (Psychology of Culture) that aspires to look deeply into the role and function of culture in human psychology, behavior, human relations, development, and learning. It will look into the adaptive function of culture and how cultures address physiological and psychological human needs. It will examine essential psychological functions and characteristics of culture based on current, empirically supported psychological theory and the relevance of culture to human development, learning, intergroup conflict, anxiety management, and the construction of meaning. It will specifically address the consequences of traumatic cultural disruption, processes of cultural recovery, dimensions of cultural variation, human universals, attributional differences, processes of colonization and decolonization, within group variation, the relationship between culture and ecology, and the relevance of these factors to educational policy and practice. *A Psychology of Culture* emerges from graduate level courses (e.g., "cross cultural counseling," "clinical work with diverse populations," "psychology of culture") taught by the author as well as direct experience providing educational, clinical, and counseling services to diverse populations in varying locations.

Honolulu, HI, USA

Michael B. Salzman

Contents

Chapter 1
Definitions and Perspectives

What is "culture?"
What role does culture play in human life and in the human condition?
What does culture emerge from?
Is culture an adaptation?
Does culture make survival more probable?
Why do people fight and die in defense of culture?
Do cultures address core human needs resident in the human condition?
What human needs are addressed by culture?
What aspects of the human condition provoke cultural construction and defense?
What is at stake when cultures are threatened, disrupted, shattered or traumatized?
What universal processes and needs are mediated by culture?
How and why do cultures change?
What is universal, culture specific and idiosyncratic in the human condition?
How do cultures differ?
How do cultures converge?
How can the positive potentials of intercultural relations be nourished?
How can the negative and destructive potentials of intercultural relations be managed?
Aren't we all alike?
What is "culture" anyway?

The Jainist story (Matilal, 1981) of the elephant and the blind men may be illustrative of the problem of defining the construct.

1.1 Elephant and the Blind Men

Once upon a time, there lived six blind men in a village. One day the villagers told them, "Hey, there is an elephant in the village today."

M.B. Salzman, *A Psychology of Culture*, International and Cultural Psychology,
https://doi.org/10.1007/978-3-319-69420-7_1

They had no idea what an elephant is. They decided, "Even though we would not be able to see it, let us go and feel it anyway." All of them went where the elephant was. Every one of them touched the elephant.

"Hey, the elephant is a pillar," said the first man who touched his leg.

"Oh, no! It is like a rope," said the second man who touched the tail.

"Oh, no! It is like a thick branch of a tree," said the third man who touched the trunk of the elephant.

"It is like a big hand fan" said the fourth man who touched the ear of the elephant.

"It is like a huge wall," said the fifth man who touched the belly of the elephant.

"It is like a solid pipe," Said the sixth man who touched the tusk of the elephant.

They began to argue about the elephant and every one of them insisted that he was right. It looked like they were getting agitated. A wise man was passing by and he saw this. He stopped and asked them, "What is the matter?" They said, "We cannot agree to what the elephant is like." Each one of them told what he thought the elephant was like. The wise man calmly explained to them, "All of you are right. The reason every one of you is telling it differently because each one of you touched the different part of the elephant. So, actually the elephant has all those features what you all said." "Oh!" everyone said. There was no more fight. They felt happy that they were all right.

The moral of the story is that there may be some truth to what someone says depending on the point of view of the observer. Sometimes we can see that truth and sometimes not because they may have different perspectives which we may not share. So, rather than arguing like the blind men, we should acknowledge the probability that there are multiple perspectives possible for any observation. We can acknowledge that one may have their reasons for their perspective and consider "Maybe you have your reasons." This way the potential for argument and conflict is reduced as we may strive to take the perspective of another. In Jainism, it is explained that truth can be stated in seven different ways. This broad view of truth teaches tolerance towards others and their viewpoints. Jainists claim that this allows for harmonious living with the people of different thinking. This is known as the Syadvada, Anekantavada, or the theory of Manifold Predictions (Matilal, 1981).

Such is the problem of definition. This book strives for the most inclusive way of describing this complex and elusive construct. There are many definitions from varied perspectives of the elephant in question that is "culture." Faulkner, Baldwin, Lindsley, and Hecht (2006) thought they could identify as many as 300 definitions of culture across disciplines that were clustered around six themes. Scholars have approached the study of culture in the thematic terms of structures, functions and processes (Smith, Fischer, Vignoles, & Bond, 2013). This volume will, after surveying varying definitions and conceptions, examine how cultures address the physiological and psychological needs of cognitively complex and anxiety prone human beings. It will consider essential needs embedded in the human condition itself.

Karl Marx famously proposed "from each according to his abilities, to each according to his needs" (1886). The underlying theme of this book is that humans are motivated to address their needs as they perceive them, that human problems may be prevented by satisfying human needs and that cultures evolve and adapt to address human psychological and physiological needs as are defined by our natures and the demands of the ecologies from which they arise and adapt.

The question then is what do humans truly need? There are varying perspectives on this question that will be considered in the course of this examination.

1.2 Culture as the Software of the Mind (Hofstede)

For Hofstede (2001) culture is the collective programming of the mind that distinguishes the members of one group or category of people from another. This programming may be considered socialization (Triandis, 1994). It is a collective phenomenon, because it is at least partly shared with people who live or lived within the same social environment, which is where it was learned. Culture is learned, not inherited. It derives from a people's interaction with a physical and psychosocial ecological environment, not from one's genes. While humans essentially possess the same neurological "hardware" groups of humans tend to differ across cultures in values, norms guiding behavior, ways of acting and interacting, attributions of meaning and what is important in life. All cultural groups have rules guiding and governing behavior but these rules and guiding norms often tend to differ across cultures because humans need to know how to *act* and *be* based on what is necessary to adapt to the demands of a particular ecological niche or context thus fulfilling an adaptive function by tending to make survival more probable. It follows that ecological change motivates culture change as cultures have been described as the highest form of human adaptation (Becker, 1971). All humans think (a function of the "hardware") but do we think alike (software)? We all interpret behaviors of others and the situations we encounter because accurate interpretations and attributions serve the ecological and existential demands of survival. Do we tend to interpret behaviors and attribute meanings to them in the same ways or do these interpretations and attributions tend to vary across groups of people relating to various ecologies, histories, geographies, and economies? This cultural variation is referred to as the "software" of the mind (Hofstede, Hofstede, & Minkov, 2010).

As with advances in computer technology this software needs updating to relate adaptively to external demands. Such ecological demands provoke cultural change (the "software") as indicated in the work of Greenfield (2009), Maynard & Greenfield (2008) and Greenfield, Maynard, and Childs (2003) with Zincatec Mayan children in Chiapas Mexico. In this case, under the pressures of globalization and commercialization child socialization patterns have been observed to change in order to support behaviors adaptive to new circumstance. Whereas weaving was traditionally taught though careful guidance with detail-oriented representation and imitation in a conservative subsistence economy the influence of cash, globalization and commercialization provoked a change toward more independent activity involving individual creativity in the development of novel weaving patterns. In this case we can see evidence of the adaptive function of culture and culture change (Greenfield, Maynard, & Marti, 2009) in response to ecological and social change. In the U.S. debates and discussions about educational policy and reform articulate educational goals as enabling youth to "compete." One may wonder why this seems to be the goal of educational policy. One explanation, favored by this examination, is that the ability to compete in the dominant ecology is responsive to the demands of global capitalism and the ideology of market fundamentalism. This ultimate goal addresses the demands of the ecological context called "globalization." Thus the elevation of the ability to compete is responsive to the current ecological context defined by the exigencies of a hegemonic economic system requiring that people acquire the skills, knowledge, and behaviors required to successfully compete in a world of "winners" and "losers." Such a system seems to guarantee large numbers of people "losing" in the grand competition thus falling into states of marginalization and dislocation. The existence of such consequences has produced motivations to seek alternative systems and ideologies to support their psychological needs. The dislocations produced by previous periods of wrenching change (i.e., industrialization) fueled the development of alternative systems such as fascism and communism (Salzman, 2001a) or today, the apparently seductive propaganda of those that call themselves the Islamic State. These ideologies appeal to the human need for perceived significance, that one's life has meaning and that one is a valued part of something larger and more enduring than the self (Kruglanski et al., 2013).

1.3 Culture as Shared Meanings and Interpretations

Rohner (1984) proposed that the essence of culture is the shared meanings and interpretations of the world around us by a group of people. These shared meanings and attributions mediate and moderate our experience with the behaviors of others and the situations in which they occur. Shweder (1991) proposed that due to the principle of existential uncertainty humans are, from birth, motivated to extrapolate meanings from the events, situations environments with which we interact. The same event may tend to be interpreted differently by varied groups and the individuals constituting those groups (Albert, 1983; Salzman, 1990, 1991). This is important because as cognitive therapy indicates we do not simply react to behaviors and situations we respond to our interpretation of these stimuli. Our behaviors respond to the meanings we attribute to situations and behaviors. We may therefore consider culture as a system of shared learned meanings by a population that is transmitted from one generation to the next. As cultures adapt to specific experiences and ecologies those aspects of a culture that have worked in terms of addressing and satisfying essential human needs (i.e., physiological survival and psychological equanimity) tend to be transmitted across generations through the socialization process. In this sense we may consider that culture may be partially defined as our understanding of what has worked in the past. This transmission of cultural knowledge and skills across generations address the basic physiological needs addressed by Maslow (1954), as they are manifest in the specific ecological niche from which that knowledge emerged thereby intended to make survival more probable.

1.4 Culture as "What Has Worked in the Past" (Triandis)

Anthropologists have offered compelling and enduring definitions of culture. Herskovits (1955) had defined culture as the human-made part of the environment. The human-made-part of the environment consists of *physical* (e.g., tools, bridges, educational systems, religious institutions) as well as *subjective* elements (e.g., beliefs, attitudes, norms, values). Kluckhohn (1954) proposed that culture is to society is what memory is to an individual. It is the memory of what has "worked in the past" that has made survival more probable. It consists of what "has worked" in the experience of a group of people facing the demands of life in a particular time and place so it was seen as worth transmitting to peers and descendants across generations (Triandis & Gelfand, 2012).

The idea that culture is "what has worked in the past" is supported by other definitions of culture cited in the literature such as:

- "By culture we mean all those historically created designs for living, explicit and implicit, rational, irrational, and non-rational, which exist at any given time as potential guides for the behavior of men" (Kluckhohn & Kelly, 1945).
- "Culture consists of patterns, explicit and implicit, of and for behavior acquired and transmitted by symbols, constituting the distinctive achievements of human groups, including their embodiments in artifacts; the essential core of culture consists of traditional (i.e. historically derived and selected) ideas and especially their attached values; culture systems may, on the one hand, be considered as products of action, and on the other as conditioning elements of further action" (Kroeber & Kluckhohn, 1952).

- "Culture is the shared knowledge and schemes created by a set of people for perceiving, interpreting, expressing, and responding to the social realities around them" (Lederach, 1995, p. 9).
- "A culture is a configuration of learned behaviors and results of behavior whose component elements are shared and transmitted by the members of a particular society" (Linton, 1945, p. 32).
- "Culture...consists in those patterns relative to behavior and the products of human action which may be inherited, that is, passed on from generation to generation independently of the biological genes" (Parson, 1949, p. 8).

Triandis (1994) emphasized that cultures arise and adapt to an ecological context consisting of a physical environment, climate, resources (or lack of them), land, fauna and flora. Triandis offered this conceptualization and theoretical framework to study and understand the relationship among ecology, culture and behavior. The relationships needn't be considered unidirectional but interactive.

$$\text{Ecology} \rightarrow \text{Culture} \rightarrow \text{Socialization} \rightarrow \text{Personality} \rightarrow \text{Behavior}$$

The ecological environment makes it possible for certain behaviors to lead to rewards and others to negative consequences. In this sense "culture" might be defined in behaviorist terms as a schedule of reinforcements. It follows that ecological change (i.e., climate change, globalization processes) requires a cultural shift if culture is to fulfill its adaptive function. He notes that in ecologies where people depend on hunting and gathering cultural adaptations are quite different from ecologies where people depend on agriculture and farming. Such differences require different behavioral and attitudinal responses in order to survive in the context. So in this sense culture may be seen as a set of reinforcement schedules (Skinner, 1981) as well as an adaptive response to the demands of a particular ecological niche or reality. Triandis and Gelfand (2012) describe ecological correlates of cultural differences such as the consequences of abundance or scarcity of resources affecting attitudes towards perceived in-groups and out-groups. They note that when resources are abundant there is a greater tendency towards individualism and looseness (loose adherence to norms) whereas when resources are scarce and cultures are relatively isolated from other cultures people are required to work cooperatively with each other while under the behavioral requirements of strict norms often rigorously enforced.

Individualism and collectivism are among the most researched variables in cross-cultural psychology. Triandis and Gelfand (2012) summarize important literature relating to the association of ecology and culture regarding these constructs. For example, collectivism most frequently occurs in agricultural societies. Rural samples are more collectivist than urban samples. Religious samples are more collectivist than secular samples. Cultural homogeneity and population density increase the probability of collectivism. The lower social classes, in all societies, are more collectivist than the upper classes. Thus, in countries with high levels of inequality there is much within nation variability in culture, with the lower classes tending toward collectivism and the upper classes toward individualism. When the ecology requires interdependence this increases the probability of collectivism. Conjunctive tasks (that require all members of the group to contribute) increase collectivism. It follows that when the demands of the ecology change cultures are moved to adapt to those changes. "Globalization" may well be such a change as it may well be the meta-context of our time stimulating cultural change in order to meet core human needs. This may be why interdisciplinary scholar and cultural anthropologist Ernest Becker (1971) suggested that culture is the highest form of human adaptation as it serves to support the physiological survival and psychological equanimity of its adherents. When culture's fail to adequately address these needs due to ecological change cultural change or collapse may ensue. This may take the form of religious conversion and/or psychological trauma (Salzman, 2001a, 2001b, 2008).

The ecology that culture adapts to may be psychological as well as physical. A people's history their interpretation of it is also context and therefore may be considered ecological. All peoples have histories and those histories often include traumatic events. These traumatic events often spawn foundational narratives that are told and retold across generations. Historical narratives concerning humiliation are particularly potent in their influence on their interpretation of current realities.

The Passover story of the exodus from slavery is told every year in the Passover Seder. The author recalls his role as the youngest son in the asking of the "four questions" beginning with "why is this night different from all other nights?" The father answers these questions as the Passover story of liberation from slavery is told and retold across the generations. The Passover narrative and the four questions and answers it poses teach lessons on who to be and how to act in the world. It teaches of the bitterness of oppression (i.e., why we serve "bitter herbs" to remind us of the bitterness of slavery), it teaches adherents to be kind to the "stranger" because "we were strangers." Members of the culture may or not internalize those teachings depending on personal and situational factors but they are explicitly present in the teachings of the story. They are part of the "Roadmap for Living" that cultures provide. So it is with the Easter story, the "Long Walk" of the Navajo and many other foundational narratives. The Jewish holocaust, the African slave trade, the horror of the institution of slavery, lynchings and manifold oppression form a psychological context and ecology that informs and shapes culture as it responds to core questions and concerns discussed below.

1.5 Culture Is a Set of Schedules of Reinforcement (Skinner, 1981)

Kluckhohn (1956) states, "neither a society or an individual will survive unless behavior makes a certain minimum of sense in terms of environmental demands" (p. 962). Since culture offers rules of conduct, customs, ideas and ways of being that, if adopted are likely to bring positive consequence, (i.e., praise instead of blame) from the social and physical context (sustenance instead of hunger) we may interpret this in behaviorist terms. Obey the rules of the culture and positive reinforcement will likely occur. This is part of the socialization process. As culture responds to the demands of the ecological niche from which it arises (Keller & Lamm, 2005) behavior and ways of being are subject to the contingencies of reinforcement imposed by the environment. Those behaviors and ways of being that make survival more probable are reinforced or selected for transmission to the next generation thereby passing on to generations "what has worked in the past (Triandis & Gelfand, 2012)." Thus cultures serve an adaptive function enhancing the probability of physiological survival in the particular ecological niche from which they arose.

1.6 Culture as the "Human-Made" Part of the Human Environment (Herskovits, 1955)

1.6.1 Culture as a Psychological Defense Against the "Terror" Inherent in the Human Condition

Culture may be thought of as a meaning system that addresses the essential existential questions of life as well as providing values to live by and a way to *be* (Becker, 1971). At the root of our consideration of the question of culture, what it is and what functions it may serve in the life of human beings, we must first consider the human condition itself. Consequently, this book takes an existential perspective on culture. That is, how does "culture" address core human concerns that are rooted in the human condition itself Maslow, 1943, 1968, 1970a, 1970b).

Mortality is a human universal and an essential human concern (Yalom, 1980) but cultures address this fact in varied ways through ritual, ceremony and belief. Humans, according to Becker (1971, 1973) and Terror Management theorists and researchers (see Greenberg, Solomon, & Pyszczynski, 1997) propose the humans have an existential problem unique to the species. That is, we are mortal and we know it. This is the "terror" referred to in Terror Management Theory (TMT). It is a terror that, if un-buffered or unmediated would leave us paralyzed by anxiety and unable to function. They suggest that culture serves as a psychological defense against this uniquely human problem. As Sam Keen writes in his preface to Becker's classic *Denial of Death* (Becker, 1973) "Since the main task of human life is to become heroic and transcend death, every culture must provide its members with an intricate symbolic system that is covertly religious. This means that ideological conflicts between cultures are essentially battles between immortality projects, holy wars (p. xiii)" In this sense, intercultural conflicts may be seen as a conflict between competing immortality ideologies. This perspective will be further explored and will serve as the conceptual and theoretical framework employed for this examination of culture and its psychological and adaptive functions. The role of culture as addressing core human needs both physiological and psychological is the organizing theme of this presentation.

Becker (1971, 1973) saw culture as a structure of rules, customs and ideas that serve as a vehicle for heroism and self-esteem construction. In the psychoanalytic tradition he noted that the task for the ego is to navigate in its world without anxiety or with manageable anxiety. Since humans can reflect on the future and inevitable death this is a significant task. This fundamental human problem is a result of our relatively highly developed cognitive abilities makes us aware that we cannot fulfill our basic biological motive to live and continue existence. This is the *terror inherent in the human condition* to which Terror Management Theory (TMT) refers and this aspect of the human condition motivates culture formation, maintenance, defense and conflict.

Culture, in this view, manages anxiety by offering just those rules, customs, codes of conduct and ways of being that place right actions at the disposal of anxiety prone human beings. By believing in the cultural worldview and seeing oneself as living up to the rules, customs, values, and ways of acting and being (i.e., personality characteristics) self-esteem may be constructed. The term "self-esteem" may have been trivialized by misapplication but it is a vital psychological resource because of its anxiety-buffering functions (Greenberg et al., 1992). Anxiety is inherent in the human condition. Since anxiety and self-esteem are inversely related the individual and collective construction of self-esteem is a source of motivation that has consequence. "Self-esteem" from the perspective of this book is the conviction that one is of value in a meaningful world and self-esteem can only be constructed from a world of meaning. Culture, as indicated infuses the world with meaning by its descriptive and prescriptive functions. One achieves the conviction that one is of value in meaningful world ("self-esteem") by believing or having faith in a cultural or religious world-view and seeing oneself as achieving its standards. In a materialist cultural worldview, for example, the standards of value are material. In such a situation where the individual buys into this worldview and believes in its standards of value those with the most money and material wealth should enjoy psychological equanimity with high self-esteem and managed anxiety. Accordingly, the poor, marginalized and those without material resources would find themselves in a state of anxiety and low self regard in such a system. As previously indicted a solution to this dilemma may lie in the adoption of a different cultural worldview that allows for self-esteem construction. In this light one can consider the historical attraction of communism and the current manifestations of religious fundamentalism where one can achieve a sense of historical and even cosmic heroism in service of the divine or to a current of history that extends beyond an individual's mortality. Who among us does not want to be a person of value, a person seen as significant in a world of meaning?

For TMT theorists and researchers (see Greenberg et al., 1997) the often trivialized construct of self-esteem means that the human sees him/herself as having value in a world of meaning and self-esteem may be seen as a vital psychological resource that is constructed culturally. The individual, by believing and by living up to prescribed cultural standards one can earn that vital psychological resource called self-esteem, which gives the ego a steady buffer against the rumbling anxiety that lies at the foundation of the human condition. Becker (1971) thought that "one crucial function of culture is to make *continued* self-esteem" possible thus allowing the individual to act adaptively with anxiety (the "terror" resident and inherent in the human condition) managed. The great Alfred Adler considered self-esteem to be the dominant human motive as reflected in his statement that "The supreme law of life is this: the sense of worth of the self shall not be allowed to be diminished" (in Ansbacher & Ansbacher, 1946, p. 358). So if one crucial function of culture is to make *continued* self-esteem possible it addresses a core human need by managing the "terror" inherent in the human condition.

There is ample experimental evidence that self-esteem is inversely related to anxiety. For example, Greenberg et al. (1992), tested this relationship experimentally in three separate published studies assessing the proposition that self-esteem serves an anxiety-buffering function. In Study 1, it was hypothesized that raising self-esteem would reduce anxiety in response to vivid images of death. In support of this hypothesis, subjects who received positive personality feedback reported less anxiety in response to a video about death than did neutral feedback Ss. In Studies 2 and 3, it was hypothesized that increasing self-esteem would reduce anxiety among individuals anticipating painful shock. Consistent with this hypothesis, both success and positive personality feedback reduced subject's physiological arousal in response to subsequent threat of shock. Thus, the researchers suggest that converging evidence of an anxiety-buffering function of self-esteem was obtained. This is consistent with a body of experimental evidence indicating that threats to self-esteem generate anxiety that produces a variety of defensive responses (Bennett & Holmes, 1975; Burish & Houseton, 1979; Leary, Barnes, & Griebel, 1986) and that the use of those strategies reduces anxiety in response to self-esteem threat. Evidence also suggests that experimentally raised self-esteem minimizes anxiety when subjects are exposed to threatening stimuli. Thus there is ample evidence that self-esteem serves as an anxiety buffer. It serves a psychological defense constructed culturally by having faith in a cultural worldview and seeing oneself as living up to its standards. It is proposed that the human condition itself generates an existential threat (Jonas & Fritsehe, 2013) and resultant anxiety that rumbles in the background of our daily existence. When the defense is threatened or weakened people experience the "terror" and seek to reduce the intensity of this highly aversive state by whatever means available if they cannot construct self-esteem by meeting the standards of value their cultures prescribe. Such compensatory efforts at anxiety reduction may be extremely destructive (i.e., alcohol abuse and its consequences).

The relationship between the anxiety ("terror") inherent in the human condition, culture, meaning and self-esteem lies at the core of this analysis as self-esteem is a cultural construction and rumbling slightly below our consciousness is our existential dilemma that was previously described. If the meaning and belief system that is culture is threatened, then TMT would predict that weakening this structure should increase death-thought accessibility (DTA) the ultimate source of our existential dilemma. Schimel, Hayes, Williams, and Jahrig (2007) tested the hypothesis that if the cultural worldview protects people from thoughts about death, then weakening or challenging this structure should increase death-thought accessibility (DTA). They conducted five studies testing this (DTA) hypothesis. They found that threatening Canadian participants' cultural values (vs. those of another culture) increased DTA on a word-fragment completion task; that when participants could dismiss the threat, DTA remained low; that worldview threat increased DTA relative to accessibility for negative and neutral content. Response latencies to death, negative, and neutral content were measured; that the DTA effect emerged independently of the arousal of anger or anxiety and that participants with a pro-creation (vs. pro-evolution) worldview had higher DTA after reading an anti-creation article. The increase in DTA is important because they motivate terror management defenses such as in-group favoritism and out-group derogation, distancing, demonizing and even aggressing (McGregor et al., 1998) on an "other" who does not support one's worldview. The implications for intercultural relations of the activation of terror management defenses are serious and will be further explored in a later chapter.

The self-esteem anxiety buffer, constructed by meeting the standards of a believed in an internalized or customized cultural worldview allows anxiety prone human creatures to navigate and function in a wondrous and terrifying existence with anxiety managed and adaptive action more probable. In this sense culture directly addresses a core human need.

So the prescription for conduct free of anxiety is to choose the "right thing to do (Becker, 1971, p. 79)." This prescriptive function of culture of how to be and how to act in the world addresses a common human problem. As with other common human problems, cultures vary in these prescriptions. These prescriptions are often very explicit. The Buddhist solution to this problem is to define a worldview (i.e., life is suffering due to attachment and desire) and offer the clear prescription for "doing the right thing" known as the Eightfold Path. Two of these paths are "Right Action" and "Right Thought." The Eightfold Path seems to offer clear guidance to the fundamental existential questions of *how to be* and *what to do* or *how to act* in this wondrous and terrifying existence.

Therefore, from this point of view, culture serves a vital psychological function to manage the terror inherent in the human condition through the construction of self-esteem defined as the conviction that one is of value in a meaningful world. It does this by offering a worldview describing the nature of the world and human life and prescriptions or standard that one may achieve or not in the context of the believed worldview. What happens when a cultural worldview is smashed, shattered or discredited? What happens when the cultural worldview is believed but one doesn't see oneself as achieving its standards? From this perspective we may infer that culture serves as a psychological defense against the terror inherent in the human condition.

1.7 Culture as a "Roadmap for Living"

In 1998 the author attended the Congress of the International Association of Cross-Cultural Psychology (IACCP). As is customary the "host culture" presented aspects of their cultural traditions. After days of sophisticated and complex sessions regarding what culture is and its psychological characteristics a Native American Elder (host culture of conference) said simply and profoundly "my culture is my roadmap for living." The elegance of this definition struck the author as crystallizing all that I had heard and as this volume seeks to identify how culture addresses core human needs and concerns I wondered "do we need a road map for living?" Is this a human need? Does culture serve as a solution to the problems of living? Do we need to know how to live? Do we need to know how to be? Absent a "roadmap" what are we to do in response to our existential condition that includes an awareness of our mortality and the inevitability of our physical annihilation that may occur at any time?

The experience of indigenous peoples with contact with the West and its consequences is similar and was devastating. Across great variations of geography and genetic endowment indigenous peoples such as Tongans, Samoans, Native Hawaiians, Native Americans, Alaska Natives, Australian Aboriginals, Maoris and others have experienced contact with the West followed by dramatic depopulation due to imported diseases for which Native peoples had little immunity from. The resultant trauma, culture loss and suppression contributed to a constellation of negative health and well-being statistics. In response, movements for cultural recovery and reconstruction have appeared in dynamic form around the world (Salzman & Halloran, 2004). In Alaska in the 1980s Inupiaq Elders became concerned with culture loss and its consequences and launched a movement (Inupiat Ilitquisiat) to identify core values and answers to the questions of how to be and how to live. It is summed up as Inupiat (the "real people") Ilitqusiat ("that which make us who we are"). The Yup'ik people (Napoleon, 1996) expressed their roadmap for living as *Yuuyaraq* or the Way of the Human Being both offer explicit guidelines for how to *be* a human being or a "real person." These roadmaps identify and offer explicit values to live by. TMT would suggest that belief in these worldviews and the achievement of its standards of value should provide an anxiety buffer against the terror inherent in human existence and explains why cultural recovery movements have been and are occurring among indigenous peoples around the world.

The assault on the people's culture and its consequences are particularly germane in this examination of the role of culture in addressing core human needs. Among the many losses experienced by indigenous peoples the loss of cultural ontological prescriptions leaves people rudderless in the world and in life and facing the an awesome, terrifying (and wondrous) reality and existence without an anxiety buffer.

The perspective of this book acknowledges and is informed by all of the above definitions but is most persuaded by the idea of culture being a "roadmap" for living needed by anxiety prone cognitively complex human beings that are faced with "terror" inherent in the human condition. The role of culture in addressing human physiological and psychological needs and the idea of culture being "A Roadmap for Living" subsumes most of the definitions of culture described previously and shall be the central organizing principle of this book. The overarching perspective of this book is to begin with elements of the human condition itself and the core existential concerns that emerge from it.

1.8 Samoan Culture and Fa'aSamoa: An Example of a "Roadmap for Living"

A Samoan "roadmap for living" is embodied in Fa'aSamoa or the Samoan Way. Within Polynesia, the Samoan Islands boast a thriving culture despite the pressures of globalization and modernization. The Samoan "Roadmap for Living" is called the Fa'aSamoa that literally means "the Samoan Way." As the "Way to be a Human Being" is described by Yuyuraq (Napoleon, 1996) was the Yup'ik people's roadmap for living, Fa'aSamoa dictates the rules, and the standards to be followed if one is to be a Samoan. It is a prescription for indigenous life; a manual that provides gratification for its subscribers. The Fa'aSamoa means to eat, walk, talk, breathe, and live Samoan. All of the customs and traditions serve to perpetuate the Fa'aSamoa (Simanu, 2002). For Samoans the Fa'aSamoa is an inherited endowment; an innate understanding of their *tofi* a God given gift that emphasizes the responsibility of every Samoan to the Samoan heritage (Tamasese, 2009). For every Samoan person, his or her *tofi* is to preserve the Fa'aSamoa. Research and conversations with Samoan elders who are also professors of Samoan oratory and culture at the University of Hawai'i at Manoa identified five pillars that represent the core standards of Fa'aSamoa; land, language, the *matai* (chief) system and respect. *Tofi* stresses the obligation of every Samoan to meet these standard within the cultural worldview of Samoan people. These pillars entail a connection and respect for the land, knowledge and understanding of the *matai* system and service to the family and community.

1.9 Yup'ik Culture and "the Way of the Human Being": An Example of a "Roadmap for Living"

In the 1990s Harold Napoleon, a Yup'ik wrote a powerful, influential and explanatory manuscript from prison that resonated across Native Alaska. It was called Yuuyaraq: The Way of the Human Being (1996). It was a clear description of what will later be described as "cultural trauma" which may be understood as a collapse or disruption of a world of meaning that sustained a people. In Napoleon's thought such a collapse occurred with the introduction of foreign diseases for which Native peoples had little immunity. The resulting anguish, bewilderment and death precipitated a cultural collapse as the traditional cultural solutions failed to halt the devastation. Absent a coherent and functional meaning system a sense of personal value cannot be constructed and there is no defense against the existential anxiety described by TMT. Absent this psychological defense the individual and people do what they can to, at least temporarily, assuage the negative state of anxiety and despair. Alcohol is one such devastating temporary "solution." However, it is one that brings more tragedy, abuse, and grief. The notion of "cultural trauma" and the motive to recover or reconstruct lost or fragmented culture will be elaborated on later but for now we focus on the ontologically prescriptive function of cultures.

Napoleon (1996) describes the world of meaning that was shattered by the "Great Death" resulting from the epidemics that devastated the Yup'ik people. The world of meaning was the "old" culture that has physically and psychologically sustained the people for millennia. He described it in this way:

> "They were ruled by customs, traditions, and spiritual beliefs of their people and shaped by these and their environment: the tundra, the river and the Bering Sea. Their world was complete; it was a very old world. They called it *Yuuyaraq*, 'the way of being a human being.' Although unwritten, this way can be compared to behavior between parents and children, grandparents and grandchildren, mothers in law and daughters and sons-in-law. It determined which members of the community could talk with each other and which members could tease each other. It defined acceptable behavior for all members of the community. It outlined the protocol for every and any situation that human beings might find themselves in" (pp. 4–5).

Such is the prescriptive function of culture as it responds to the core questions we all confront of how to be and how to act in this life to perceive oneself as having value in a meaningful world. It offers a roadmap for living in an awesome, wondrous and terrifying existence. Readers may consider their response to the question "What is my roadmap for living?"

1.10 Personal Note

In the early 1980s the author lost both of his parents. This was a normal development as the parents preceded the children and the "children" were adult. However, loss and grief are wrenching and disorienting experiences for most people and this was true for the author who was socialized in Jewish culture. A high cultural value in Jewish culture is education and the pursuit of education for its own sake is greatly supported by this cultural value. The author, raw with grief and suffering the disorientation of a changed subjective world went back to school. The Jewish jokes about "my son the doctor" rang true as I entered a Ph.D. program. The pursuit of the Ph.D. was of value in itself and the achievement of this goal was of the highest value. In this sense the author followed the roadmap of what to do and how to be in this life. Anxiety was assuaged, depression lifted and the author was able to pass through the pain of grief and the disruption of the world embedded in the warm approval of this high cultural norm and value. People have subjective responses to grief and they are often destructive as in the use of drink and drug to numb the pain. But as stated, culture provides just those rules and customs, goals of conduct that place right actions automatically at the individual's disposal. By acting in accordance with those rules, norms, goals and customs the individual who buys into the culture may construct self-esteem or a sense of significance and value. The achievement of a sense of having value in a world of meaning serves as a buffer against anxiety (the "terror inherent in human existence") thereby facilitating adaptive action. There is a compelling literature indicating the inverse relationship between anxiety and self-esteem. The act of learning in Jewish culture is valued. The achievement of becoming an "educated person" brings praise, support and validation from the culture that may be internalized by the individual. This was so in the case of the author and his grief that he was able to pass through relatively unscathed.

In summary, there are multiple perspectives on what "culture" is and the role it plays in human existence. This volume considers many of these perspectives but emphasizes the notion of culture as a psychological defense against the "terror" inherent in the human condition by providing a "roadmap" for living contextualized by a worldview and standards of value and virtue that if achieved provides for the construction of that which is called self-esteem if one believes in or has faith in a cultural worldview. At the root of this conception is the human condition itself. We are anxiety prone creatures who are aware on some level that we face ultimate and inevitable physical annihilation. This uncomfortable fact requires beliefs, defenses and compensations to allow for us to function in the face of this awareness. Cultures infuse the world with meaning and in such a world it is possible to construct self-esteem or the sense that one has value in a meaningful world. It motivates the desire to belong to, contribute to, or create something that extends beyond our mortal lives. A "roadmap for living" provided by cultures indicates a pathway to the construction of self-esteem which has been demonstrated to buffer oneself against anxiety and most specifically existential anxieties. By contributing or perceiving oneself to part of something larger and more enduring than self one may, according to belief systems, achieve a sense of literal or symbolic immortality. It may be the promise of paradise through "martyrdom" or contributing to the continuation of the "American Way" or more tangibly to the production and development of children. Birth and death are truly human universals. How we address these universals vary across cultures and become a question of beliefs. When these beliefs differ among groups of people in certain conditions bloody conflict may ensue. In this sense cultural differences may represent clashing immortality ideologies where the "other" is distanced from, derogated, demonized and even annihilated to prove the rightness of one's cultural and/or religious worldview. History is replete with such conflicts and there is no shortage of evidence to support this tendency.

Cultures, then, provide for the opportunity to construct a world of meaning to act in ways that enhance the notion that on has value and significance in a meaningful world. This belief, self-esteem, is a proposed as a universal psychological need that is constructed differently across cultures. One may buy into a particular culture entirely, partially or not at all. Still, the need remains. One may sample elements from a particular cultural worldview or one may idiosyncratically construct one from elements of different cultures. In any case one must believe in it and see oneself as achieving its standards of value and being in order to construct an anxiety buffer. Absent such an anxiety buffer a person becomes subject to existential terror rooted in our awareness of our mortality and our inability to fulfill our basic biological motive to continue existence.

Certainly, the human condition contains more than existential terror. It also allows for the joy of wonder, growth and creativity. It is plausible that one may deal with the terror inherent in the human condition by embracing the wonder of it and the life we have.

References

Albert, R. A. (1983). The intercultural sensitizer or culture assimilator: A cognitive approach. In D. Landis & R. Brislin (Eds.), *Handbook of intercultural training* (Vol. II, pp. 186–217). New York: Pergamon.

Ansbacher, H., & Ansbacher, R. (1946). *The individual psychology of Alfred Adler*. New York: Basic Books.

Becker, E. (1971). *The birth and death of meaning* (2nd ed.). New York: Free Press.

Becker, E. (1973). *The denial of death*. New York: Free Press.

Bennett, D. H., & Holmes, D. S. (1975). Influences of denial (situational redefinition) and projection on anxiety associated with threat to self–esteem. *Journal of Personality and Social Psychology, 32*, 915–921.

Burish, T. G., & Houston, B. K. (1979). Causal projection, similarity projection, and coping with threat to self esteem. *Journal of Personality, 47*, 57–70.

Faulkner, S. L., Baldwin, J. R., Lindsley, S. L., & Hecht, M. L. (2006). Layers of meaning: An analysis of definitions of culture. In J. R. Baldwin, S. L. Faulkner, M. L. Hecht, & S. L. Lindsley (Eds.), *Redefining culture: Perspectives across the disciplines* (pp. 27–51). Mahwah, NJ: Erlbaum.

Greenberg, J., Solomon, S., & Pyszczynski, T. (1997). Terror management theory of self-esteem and cultural worldviews: Empirical assessments and conceptual refinements. In M. P. Zanna (Ed.), *Advances in experimental social psychology* (Vol. 29, pp. 61–139). San Diego, CA: Academic.

Greenberg, J., Solomon, S., Pyszczynski, T., Rosenblatt, A., Burling, J., Lyon, D., Simon, L., & Pinel, E. (1992). Why do people need self-esteem? Converging evidence that self-esteem serves an anxiety-buffering function. *Journal of Personality and Social Psychology, 63*(6), 913–922. https://doi.org/10.1037/0022-3514.63.6.913.

Greenfield, P. M. (2009). Linking social change and developmental change: Shifting pathways of human development. *Developmental Psychology, 45*, 401–418.

Greenfield, P. M., Maynard, A. E., & Childs, C. P. (2003). Historical change, cultural learning, and cognitive representation in Zinacantec Maya children. *Cognitive Development, 18*, 455–487.

Greenfield, P. M., Maynard, A. E., & Marti, F. A. (2009). Implications of commerce and urbanization for the learning environments of everyday life: A Zinacantec Maya family across time and space. *Journal of Cross-Cultural Psychology, 40*, 935–952.

Herskovits, M. J. (1955). *Cultural anthropology*. New York: Knof.

Hofstede, G. (2001). *Culture's consequences: Comparing values, behaviors, institutions and organizations across nations* (2nd ed.). Thousand Oaks, CA: Sage.

Hofstede, G., Hofstede, G. J., & Minkov, M. (2010). *Culture and organizations: Software of the mind* (3rd ed.). London: McGraw-Hill.

Jonas, E., & Fritsche, I. (2013). Destined to die but not to wage war: How existential threat can contribute to escalation or de-escalation of violent intergroup conflict. *American Psychologist, 68*, 543–558.
Keller, H., & Lamm, B. (2005). Parenting as the expression of socio-historical time: The of German individuation. *International Journal of Behavioral Development, 29*, 238–246.
Kluckhohn, C., & Kelly, W. H. (1945). The concept of culture. In R. Linton (Ed.), *The science of man in the world culture* (pp. 78–105). New York: Columbia University Press.
Kluckhohn, C. (1954). Southwestern studies of culture and personality. *American Anthropologist, 56*(4), 685–697.
Kluckhohn, C. (1956). Culture and behavior. In G. Lindsey (Ed.), *Handbook of social psychology* (Vol. II, pp. 921–976). Redding, MA: Addison-Wesley.
Kroeber, A. L., & Kluckhohn, C. (1952). *Culture: A critical review of concepts and definitions, Papers of the Peabody Museum of American Archaeology and Ethnology, Harvard University*. Cambridge, MA: The Museum.
Kruglanski, A. W., Belanger, J. J., Gelfand, M., Gunarantna, R., Hettiarachchi, M., Reinares, F., Orehek, E., Sosata, J., & Sharvit, K. (2013). Terrorism—A (self) love story: Redirecting the significance quest can end violence. *American Psychologist, 68*, 559–575. https://doi.org/10.1037/a0032615.
Leary, M. R., Barnes, B. D., & Griebel, C. (1986). Cognitive, affective, and attributional effects of potential threats to self-esteem. *Journal of Social and Clinical Psychology, 4*, 461–474.
Lederach, J. P. (1995). *Preparing for peace: Conflict transformation across cultures*. Syracuse, NY: Syracuse University Press.
Linton, R. (1945). *The cultural background of personality*. New York.
Marx, K., & Engels, F. (1886). *Manifesto of the communists*. London: International Publishing.
Maslow, A. H. (1943). A theory of human motivation. *Psychological Review, 50*(4), 370–396.
Maslow, A. H. (1954). *Motivation and personality*. New York: Harper and Row.
Maslow, A. H. (1968). *Toward a psychology of being*. New York: D. Van Nostrand.
Maslow, A. H. (1970a). *Motivation and personality*. New York: Harper & Row.
Maslow, A. H. (1970b). *Religions, values, and peak experiences*. New York: Penguin. (Original work published 1964).
Matilal, B. K. (1981). *The Central Philosophy of Jainism (Anekantavada)*, L.D. Series 79. Ahmedabad.
Maynard, A. E., & Greenfield, P. M. (2008). Women's schooling and other ecocultural shifts: A longitudinal study of historical change among the Zinacatec Maya. *Mind, Culture, and Activity, 15*, 165–175.
McGregor, H. A., Lieberman, J. D., Greenberg, J., Solomon, S., Simon, L., Arnt, J., & Pyszczynski, T. (1998). Terror management and aggression: Evidence that mortality salience motivates aggression against worldview-threatening others. *Journal of Personality and Social Psychology, 74*, 590–605.
Napoleon, H. (1996). AK: University of Alaska Fairbanks, Alaska: Native Knowledge Network.
Parson, T. (1949). *Essays in sociological theory*. Glencoe, IL: Free Press.
Rohner, R. P. (1984). Toward a conception of culture for cross-cultural psychology. *Journal of Cross-cultural psychology, 15*(2), 111–138.
Salzman, M. (1990). The construction of an intercultural sensitizer for training non-Navajo personnel. *Journal of American Indian Education, 1*, 112–118.
Salzman, M. (1991). *A Navajo intercultural sensitizer. Center for cross-cultural studies college of rural Alaska*. Fairbanks, AK: University of Alaska Fairbanks.
Salzman, M. (2001a). Globalization, culture & anxiety. *Journal of Social Distress and the Homeless, 10*(4), 337–352.
Salzman, M. (2001b). Cultural trauma and recovery: Perspectives from terror management theory. *Trauma, Violence, & Abuse, 2*(2), 172–191.
Salzman, M. B., & Halloran, M. J. (2004). Cultural trauma and recovery: Cultural meaning, self-esteem, and the re-construction of the cultural anxiety-buffer. In J. Greenberg, S. L. Koole,

& T. Pyszczynski (Eds.), *Handbook of experimental existential psychology* (pp. 231–246). New York: Guilford.
Salzman, M. B. (2008). Globalization, religious fundamentalism and the need for meaning. *International Journal of Intercultural Relations, 32*(4), 318–327.
Schimel, J., Hayes, J., Williams, T., & Jahrig, J. (2007). Is death really the worm at the core? Converging evidence that worldview threat increases death-thought accessibility. *Journal of Personality and Social Psychology, 92*(5), 789–803. https://doi.org/10.1037/0022-3514.92.5.789.
Shweder, R. A. (1991). *Thinking through culture. Expeditions in cultural psychology*. Cambridge, MA: Harvard University Press.
Simanu, A. M. (2002). *O si manu a alii: A text for the advanced study of samoan language and culture*. Hawai'i: UH Press Honolulu.
Skinner, B. F. (1981). Selection by consequences. *Science, 213*, 501–504.
Smith, P. B., Fischer, R., Vignoles, V. L., & Bond, M. H. (2013). *Understanding social psychology across cultures: Engaging with others in a changing world* (2nd ed.). London: Sage.
Tamasese, T. T. (2009). *Su'esue'e Manogi: In search of frangrance*.
Triandis, H. C. (1994). *Culture and social behavior*. New York: McGraw Hill.
Triandis, H. C., & Gelfand, M. (2012). A theory of individualism and collectivism. In P. A. M. Van Lange, A. W. Kruglanski, & E. T. Higgins (Eds.), *Handbook of social psychological theories* (Vol. 2, pp. 498–520). Los Angeles, CA: Sage.
Yalom, I. (1980). *Existential psychotherapy*. New York: Basic Books.

Chapter 2
The Human Condition

Universals (true for all), Culture Specific (true for some) and Idiosyncratic (true for one) aspects of being human (e.g., emics and etics and idiosyncratic variation within groups).
Birth, death, meaning and anxiety
Variform universals
Six common human problems and varying cultural responses

What is universally true for all humans (true for all)?
What is culturally specific to groups of people (true for some)?
What is idiosyncratic and unique in humans (true for one)?

Psychology has been relatively late in considering culture, its characteristics, and the functions it embodies in human life. Historically, psychology has imposed a western, ethnocentric perspective ("emic") on culturally diverse populations. This imposition presumed that a culturally specific western ("emic") perspective was universal ("etic") thereby holding that all who differ from these mono-culturally specified norms were "primitive", deviant, or deficient. Inherent in this imposition was the Type I error of pathologizing normative and adaptive cultural differences as well as supporting existing power relationships in society. Thanks to the enormous contributions of scholars such as Marsella, Triandis, Brislin, Berry and others psychology has acknowledged culture as an important factor in psychological and behavioral processes. Nourished by the research of these and other scholars the field of cross-cultural psychology developed rapidly and has provided new perspectives on the human condition, what is truly universal in humans and those aspects of human experience that vary culturally and idiosyncratically.

M.B. Salzman, *A Psychology of Culture*, International and Cultural Psychology,
https://doi.org/10.1007/978-3-319-69420-7_2

2.1 The Universal, Culturally Specific and Idiosyncratic Aspects of Our Humanity

How are we all alike and how do we differ? Berry (1969), drawing on the field of linguistics (Pike, 1967) contrasted two approaches to cross-cultural studies. One could start from the assumption that there are universals truths and phenomena ("true for all") and proceed accordingly until evidence is found to support the assertion of cultural differences ("true for some") between and among culturally specific populations. In contrast to the "etic" approach, one could start from an "emic" perspective where one starts from an intensive study of the distinctive characteristics of a specific cultural group where the focus is on local meanings and relies on information provided by persons within that cultural group. These approaches are associated with different epistemological traditions (Smith, Fischer, Vignoles, & Bond, 2013). Etic research is associated with positivist and post positivist epistemologies and the presumption of the existence of objective "truth" whereas emic research attends to culturally specific attributes that can only be understood in the sociocultural context they are embedded in. The imposition of an emic (culturally specific) presumed to be an etic (universal) has been termed a "pseudo-etic" that is usually imposed on the less powerful by the more powerful (Berry, 1969). It is a source of error and may be a source of or reflection of oppression.

In consideration of these questions we can assert with some confidence that all humans are born, all humans die and that these events may be viewed and addressed differentially across cultures. We can also assert that humans possess relatively sophisticated cognitive abilities and potentials that allow us to reflect on ourselves, consider our mortality and to construct meaning. We can also assert that cognitively complex humans, with their universal origins as dependent, relatively helpless and powerless organisms in an awesome and dangerous world are prone to experience anxiety. The perspective taken here is that anxiety is part of the human condition due to our awareness of our predicament, that is, the awareness of our mortality and our knowledge that we cannot fulfill our basic biological motive that is shared with all other species, to continue existence. This is our existential problem that cultures address in varied ways. What is universally true for all humans? What is (culturally specific) true for some humans? What is idiosyncratically true for the individual?

Lonner (2000) described a seven-level structure of human universals (true for all. These levels were labeled):

- Simple Universals (e.g., the absolute facticity of human aggression);
- Variform Universals (e.g., aggression takes on various forms in different cultures, but it occurs across cultures albeit in various forms of expression);
- Functional universals (societal variations that have the same social consequences, but equilibrated for local relevance);
- Diachronic universals (universals of behavior that are temporally invariant, but interpreted differently);
- Ethologically-oriented universals (those with phylogenetic, Darwinian links);

- Systematic Behavioral Universals (various subcategories in psychology, and there are many of them);
- Cocktail Party Universals (those things that all people feel but can only discuss as phenomena that defy measurement).

From the perspective of this book the first two levels described by Lonner are the most interesting and useful. We are all born and we all die. Our beliefs, practices, customs and norms vary as to how humans deal with this observable fact. What common human problems do all culture's respond to? Are all cultural specific phenomena really cultural variations on universal concerns and challenges that is, variform universals. It is important to recognize that, while psychology's relatively recent focus on culture and cultural variations is needed and most welcome we must recognize that within group (cultures) variations are likely to be at least as great as between group (culture specific) differences. Individuals from the same cultural systems may sample and internalize different aspects of the culture into their identity and style of life determined by an individual's view of view of him/herself, view of the world and unique pathway of goal striving in the context of cultural and situational influences (Ansbacher & Ansbacher, 1946). Cultures offer pathways that enable individuals within a cultural system the possibility of achieving *significance* or the conviction that one's life and person has value in a meaningful world. Cultures provide "just those rules, customs and goals of conduct that place right actions automatically at the individual's disposal" and that it is the function of self-esteem to give the ego a steady buffer against anxiety (Becker, 1971, p. 79). By providing just those rules, behavioral prescriptions and valued goals the individual maybe provided with the conviction that he or she is of value in a world of meaningful action. Maslow (1954) proposed that the conviction that one has value in a meaningful world ("self esteem") is a universal human need. Adler (see Ansbacher & Ansbacher, 1946) suggested that this feeling and conviction ("self-esteem") is in fact the dominant human motive.

The inference that a relationship (i.e., subjective culture and value differences) holds true at the individual level because it has been true at a national or macro level invites interpretative error. This has been called the "ecological fallacy." It is the false belief that the relationship between two variables (i.e., attributions and subjective culture) must be the same at different levels of analysis. Triandis and Gelfand (2012) remind us that individual level data may differ from the cultural-level data and proposed the use of different terms for data at the individual level of analysis. "Allocentrics" and "idiocentrics" were proposed as personality configurations reflecting collectivism and individualism. While many of the cognitions found in collectivist cultures may be found among allocentrics, and many of the cognitions found in individualist cultures may be found among idiocentrics, it is best to *not* assume that in collectivist cultures everybody will be allocentric. Every culture has both allocentric and idiocentric individuals. Triandis, Chan, Bhawuk, Iwao, and Sinha (1995) proposed that the best way to conceptualize such within group variation in relation to cross cultural comparisons is to think that both collectivist and individualist cognitions are present in every individual, and the tendencies are elicited by the *situation*. The fit between culture and personality have implications for personal development and adjustment. Allocentrics in collectivist cultures and idiocentrics in individualist cultures tend to be well adjusted. However, allocentrics in individualist cultures may feel that there are not enough relationships, so they are likely to join communes, unions, gangs, associations, and other groups that will increase their satisfaction with relationships. Idiocentrics in collectivist cultures are likely to look for opportunities to leave that culture, because they feel that too much conformity to in-group norms is required (Triandis & Gelfand, 2012).

The potential source of error that may result from ignoring within-group variations (the ecological fallacy) invites stereotyping an individual by his or her group identification. Cultural stereotypes may lead to serious error when applied to the level of individuals. While stereotypical generalizations may contain some truth (Allport, 1954) they may also lead to dehumanizing prejudices that confound human relationships. When cultural stereotypes are used as a provisional hypothesis as a basis for cross-cultural interactions they may serve to facilitate those interactions. However, it is essential to consider these generalizations (i.e., Native Americans do not make direct eye contact) as provisional. Cultural generalizations that may lead to stereotyping are perhaps best thought of as tendencies and our assumptions of their applicability to individuals may be treated as hypotheses to be tested by experience. An alternative approach to intercultural interactions is a culture blind perspective by assuming that what is held in common is far more significant than culture related differences. Difficulties arising from the interactions of this approach could prompt one to consider culture-level differences. One may then assess known group level cultural differences as a possible source of the difficulties. In both approaches the potential sources of error and misinterpretation must be considered and to the extent possible minimized. Above all, the error of dehumanizing the "other" into an object or stereotype must be avoided.

The functionality of stereotypes and stereotyping bears re-examination if we are to dilute or moderate their effects on prejudice formation, discrimination and ultimately dehumanization by obscuring the individual in a broad generalization about their presumptive culture, race or category.

2.2 The Functionality of Stereotypes

Salzman (2012) described the functionality of stereotyping from varied perspectives. Stereotypes are closely associated with prejudice and discrimination. They pervade people's views of their social worlds. Stereotypes are usually simple, over generalized assertions about what "they" are like. "They" are denied their individuality by having applied to them a set of beliefs about their character and propensities of behavior (Snyder & Miene, 1994). By denying "their" individuality we are ultimately denying their humanity. We see only a category. Dehumanization lies at the root of the indignities and even atrocities that humans impose on fellow humans. What needs are met and psychological functions served by the stereotypes that afflict our social perception and interpersonal behavior? Snyder and Miene (1994) describe three orientations associated with three particular functions served by stereotypes.

A *cognitive orientation* on the functionality of stereotypes suggests that humans are limited in the amount of incoming information they can process, and form stereotypes as one way to reduce the cognitive burden of dealing with a complex world. In this orientation, stereotypes serve the function of *cognitive economy* by reducing incoming data to a manageable level so as to imbue our worlds with a sense of predictability.

A *psychodynamic orientation* sees stereotypes as providing a variety of ego-defensive functions. They include the derogation of others (particularly those seen as competitors for scarce resources) and the building of self-esteem by engaging in downward social comparison. Stereotypes therefore are subjectively useful for making people feel better about themselves and less threatened by other groups of people. Therefore, in functional terms stereotypes serve the function of ego defense and protection.

A *sociocultural orientation* suggests that stereotypes serve the social function of fitting in and achieving a sense of belonging which has long been recognized as a human need (e.g., Maslow, 1987). Sherif, Harvey, White, Hood, and Sherif (1954) saw such stereotypes as functionally related to becoming a group member thereby serving a social function.

These three types of functions serve real human needs and humans are motivated to satisfy their needs as they are perceived (i.e., the need for a predictable world, the need for self-esteem, and the need to belong). Given their ubiquity and nature, stereotypes must be considered a source of error with potentially serious consequences that call for strategies to minimize their negative impact on human and intergroup relations. Pettigrew (1998) described the as the optimal sequence of contact between groups as first, *decategorization*: seeing similarity with the "other"—seeing the "other" as an individual and interaction as an interpersonal not intergroup event; second, *salient categorization* other's group made salient so the "other" seen as representative of their group in some essential way and; third *recategorization* into a larger category such as "working class" or "human race" that is inclusive ("we world") is created that includes all interactants. In this case a person's individuality, culture and universal humanity are acknowledged and the full humanity of the person is acknowledged so no dehumanization occurs and dehumanization is a prerequisite for discrimination, demonization, and atrocity. This formulation does not "deracialize" but acknowledges differences while including them in a larger formulation.

The consequences of dehumanization may range from the inconvenient to the catastrophic. As described by Zimbardo (2007), once certain groups are dehumanized or stigmatized as evil, morally inferior, and not fully human, the persecution of those groups becomes more psychologically acceptable. Restraints against aggression and violence begin to disappear. Not surprisingly, dehumanization increases the likelihood of violence and may cause a conflict to escalate out of control. Once a violence and death has occurred, it may seem even more acceptable for people to do things that they would have regarded as morally unthinkable before. The processes of dehumanization must be understood and disrupted if discrimination, exploitation, derogation, atrocity and even annihilation are to be prevented. How and under what circumstances do we dehumanize our fellow humans? The dehumanizing process may be inhibited by our steadfast conviction of the humanity of the "other" and the complex and varied potentials resident in all of us. The descent from generalizations to stereotyping to dehumanization may be a slippery slope indeed.

2.3 An Existential Perspective

This book looks at the human condition and how cultures address the needs inherent in it. Consequently, the perspective of this approach to culture is derived from the traditions of existential philosophy and, broadly speaking, psychodynamic theory. Philosopher William Barrett (1959, p. 126) defined existentialism as a "philosophy that confronts the human situation *in its totality* to ask what the basic conditions of human existence is" and how humans can establish their own meaning out of these conditions. This perspective seeks bedrock in the human condition and the existential realities that confront us and the human needs embedded in those realities. Among those needs is the centrality of the human need for meaning. Meaning has been seen to have several characteristics. A meaningful world is a predictable and orderly world. It is a perception of reliable contingencies for effective action (Arnt, Landau, Vail, & Vess, 2013). It involves expected relationships between action and its consequences. It answers the question of "why" and addresses the question of what has value. It provides a guide for living and a moral compass to assess behaviors and events. At the macro level we construct and are informed by cultural worldview that is a set of socially constructed beliefs about the origin and nature of existence. The motivation to achieve meaning can be observed in the questions of young children seeking the answer to the questions of existence they confront. They want to know "why" things are as they appear. Why are people mean? Why is the sky blue? Or as the daughter of a friend asked "Why am I crying?" These questions can be profound. When a pet or a loved one dies the child is deeply concerned about its meaning. From the very early on the child's understanding of what things *mean* emerges from a conditional sense of safety and protection from harm (Arnt et al., 2013). Meaning involves an attempt to make sense of our lives. A meaningful world is a coherent world. It is a moral world. The disintegration of meaning is essentially a disintegration of one's moral universe leaving us rudderless in a precarious existence. Do our lives make sense to us? How can we determine this? Cultures describe a world of meaning and a guide to actions and ways of being that may imbue one's perception of their lives with a sense of value and significance. Who among us does not want a life of value and significance? Culture offers pathways to the subjective perception of value and significance and value and significance can only be constructed in a meaningful world. Meaning is proposed here as a universal human need and that cultures may infuse the world with meaning. The search for meaning is proposed as a human universal where the meanings themselves that people seek and internalize may vary across cultures.

2.4 Note from the Class

The relationship of human universals (etics) and cultural relativity (emics) that address these universals was explored in the "Psychology of Culture" class that inspired this book. The proposition that culture serves as a psychological defense against the terror inherent in the human condition will be explored in depth in a later chapter but at this juncture in our discussion of human universals, culturally specific and idiosyncratic aspects of our humanity the source of this existential "terror" and our varied cultural responses to it bears mention. We are all subject to the universal fact of mortality, that is, the inescapable truth that we all face inevitable physical annihilation. This physical annihilation may occur at any time and we know this. This universal and observable fact is viewed differently across cultures and the ceremonies and rituals constructed to deal with the resultant grief reflect culturally and religiously specific beliefs about our mortality and existence. The physical fact of inevitable physical annihilation is indisputable the rest are beliefs about this fact and these vary.

Therefore, as noted, we humans have an existential problem. This problem is embedded in the human condition itself. We, like all creatures, share the powerful biological motive to live and continue existence. However, we are self-aware and possess highly sophisticated cognitive abilities that allow us to reflect on ourselves, our past and to ponder the future. Becker (1971) argued that self-awareness is the most important characteristics that distinguish humans from other creatures and that it is this capacity for self-awareness produces our existential dilemma. These advanced cognitive abilities are most likely our greatest strength as a species but they also present us with a unique existential problem….we are aware of our mortality. We know that we ultimately cannot satisfy our basic biological motive because we all face inevitable physical annihilation. This, as noted, is a universal and undeniable fact. We all are born and we all die. Our beliefs about this fact vary across cultures and individuals (Solomon, Greenberg, & Pyszczynski, 2004). This awareness is the "terror" inherent in the human condition. It is a terror that, if unmediated would lead to paralysis of action or action that may be destructive to self and others (e.g., substance abuse and related behaviors). In order to truly understand human motivation and behavior we must confront the existential realities we face and the human condition that we share (Becker, 1973). We must ask big questions like what are the basic conditions of human existence and how can humans establish their own meaning out of these conditions (Pyszczynski, Greenberg, & Koole, 2004). Yalom (1980) described existential thought as focused on the human confrontation with the fundamentals of existence. He described four basic concerns that universally influence our lives: death, freedom, existential isolation and meaning or meaninglessness. This list of existential concerns is not complete. It does not represent the totality of our concerns. As we shall see we are also concerned about how we fit into the universe, how we relate to nature and what kind of persons should we BE, and what actions have value.

All cultures develop grieving ceremonies that are rooted in beliefs about mortality and that serve an adaptive function in supporting believers through the wrenching experience of grief and loss. The "Psychology of Culture" class looked at the "cultural trauma" experienced by the indigenous peoples of Alaska as a result contact with Europeans and the resultant "great death" due to imported diseases to which the Native peoples had little resistance (Napoleon, 1996). The dramatic and stunning depopulation of the indigenous peoples throughout the world presented people with a crisis (Salzman, 2001, 2005). Indigenous healers and respected elders also died. Religious conversion followed. Traditions were lost or discredited. Explanatory ceremonies, stories, dances and songs were often lost.

The "memorial Potlatch" is a grieving ceremony used for centuries by Athabaskan people of Alaska. Elders were concerned that the healing power of this ceremony was being lost. Two respected elders who lost their son to one of the many tragic "accidents" common to the indigenous communities in Alaska decided to videotape the memorial potlatch they held for their deceased son. Their intention was to show how the Potlatch was done before the ceremony and the knowledge of the old people was lost. This culturally specific way of dealing with the universal fact of death, grief and loss may serve as a good example of a variform universal (Lonner, 2000) where the universal phenomenon of mortality is addressed in culturally specific ways. When grieving ceremonies are lost people are left with the pain and unresolved grief. It is plausible that the unresolved grief produces maladaptive responses to alleviate the pain of grief. Substance abuse is such a maladaptive response that produces more tragedy, more grief and more destructive behaviors that would seem to temporarily alleviate the grief and the trauma may be transmitted across generations and the process may continue across generations. The author believes he observed this process in Native Alaska.

At the root of the quest for universals ("etics") must be an examination the human condition itself. Humans as with all life are born and must die. What that means to people varies across cultures and belief systems. How this fact is addressed varies across cultures ("emics") and individuals. Cultures, however varied, meet the same fundamental and inescapable needs of individuals living a social life in groups. These needs will be examined in the next chapter but suffice it to say at this point we all seek to live and continue existence and the requirements of this imperative vary according to environment, situation and ecology. All cultures give their own cognitive and symbolic answers to the essential questions of What? How? Why? and When? (Kluckhohn, 1956). The answers to these questions form the basis of what we now refer to as the "cultural world view" of a people. Certainly there is variation within cultural groups. The aspects of the cultural worldview that are internalized by individuals vary across personality characteristics, situations and the saliency of the activated cultural norms (Jonas & Fritsche, 2013). Kluckhohn (1956) suggests that the underlying "genotype" of all cultures is the same while the phenotypic manifestations vary greatly in response to the environmental and ecological demands of place and time. This universality and relativity serve cultures' primary adaptive function, which is to make survival more probable (Becker, 1971).

The adaptive function of culture is captured by Kluckhohn's (1950) identification of common human problems that life demands we confront. Becker (1971) notes that one of the main reasons that cultural differences can be threatening is that despite their many varieties cultures ask and answer the same basic questions so that when different ways of life constructed around the answers to these questions come into contact they may clash on the same vital points. These vital points include core human concerns and needs. In order to properly conceptualize these issues, we must consider the human condition and the unique problems it produces that culture addresses. These include the six common human problems addressed by cultures identified by anthropologist (see Kluckhohn, 1950) are listed below with some brief commentary:

- *What is the relation of human to nature?*
- *What is the innate predisposition of humans?*
- *What types of personality are most values?*
- *What are the modes of relating to others?*
- *What kind of space-time dimension does human action take place?*

Conceptions and perceptions of time and space may differ across cultures. Human action and being are situated in such conceptions. Legendary anthropologist Clyde Kluckhohn (1954) notes that based on Hopi data, that it is "no longer the homogeneous and instantaneous timeless space of our supposed intuition" (p. 934). He understood that just as it is possible to have any number of geometries other than Euclidian, different conceptions of the universe including time and space may exist and be equally valid. Lee (1950) questions the universality of the concept of time and other concepts as having linear dimensions. She cautions that we should be careful in studying diverse cultures to avoid the unexamined assumption that human actions are based on the prediction of a lineal reality. Human action is embedded in conceptions of time and space and may be difficult to interpret absent its consideration. The answers to the problem of what kinds of space-time dimensions does human action take place may be enormously varied (Becker, 1971). Time can be cyclical and be renewed; it can be measured in moons, or by the number of reincarnations. One can exist only in physical time, here on earth; or one can extend into spiritual and eternal time and even into the time dimension of dreams. For the traditional Australian, the world of dream, legendary past and waking present are blended into synthetic experience as he lives in three worlds at once. Space may be a vaulted dome with one's island at its center and heaven touching earth on both ends of the horizon. The modern physicist may see space a spherical, extending to the furthest reaches of the universe and then curving back yet finite, unbounded but expanding where there is no center save where one stands. There are many possibilities.

- *What is the hierarchy of power in nature and society (and where do I fit into it?)*

Becker notes that this question is of the most direct concern. If we don't get this question right we fail right away in all the others. We seek to identify with the powerful and transcendent. Young children identify with their parents who represent the physical possibility of survival and the emotional needs for safety and reassurance. In times of stress and anxiety religious systems are evoked with the ultimate power for believers assigned to the divine. Our earliest experiences are infused with powerlessness and helplessness in the face of a powerful and intimidating environment. We depend on others to survive. Those who we depend on must be perceived as having sufficient power to enable the continued existence of the tiny human infant.

2.5 Personal Note

The author recalls how he idolized his father as a young boy. He was convinced his father had the ability and power to ward off danger and destruction. When it became obvious that "Dad" was not omnipotent other sources of power were considered. Adolescence saw the shift from identification with fallible "Dad" to the peer group. In elementary school he pondered questions such as whether the American flag or the Bible represented higher power. He was consumed with questions about which dinosaur was the most powerful and was extremely upset when it became apparent that the biggest dinosaur (Brontosaurus) was not the "baddest." Then he found the "baddest" which was then considered to be T-Rex. As a result of this discovery the infatuation with the previous hero (Brontosaurus) ended and the identification with T-Rex began. Ultimately, the highest apparent power is the most compelling entity for identification. Becker (1971) called religion the "quest for the ideal heroism (p. 180)" but, in the immortal words of New York Mets baseball pitcher Tug McGraw, "you gotta believe." Power is an issue for the powerless. Anxiety is a part of the human condition. We humans have an existential problem. We are doomed to inevitable physical annihilation and we know it. Humans seek a solution to this problem and cultures provide such solutions. These solutions vary but the problem may be seen as universal. Our awareness of our inevitable physical annihilation and its meaning is a core human concern.

What do humans need?

References

Allport, G. (1954). *The nature of prejudice*. Reading, MA: Addison-Wesley.

Ansbacher, H., & Ansbacher, R. (1946). *The individual psychology of Alfred Adler*. New York: Basic Books.

Arnt, J., Landau, M. J., Vail, K. E., & Vess, M. (2013). An edifice for enduring personal value: A terror management perspective on the human quest for multilevel meaning. In K. D. Markman, T. Proulx, & M. J. Lindberg (Eds.), *The psychology of meaning* (pp. 49–69). Washington, DC: American Psychological Association.

Barrett, W. (1959, November 21). What is existentialism, *Saturday Evening Post*, pp. 45, 126, 129–130.

Becker, E. (1971). *The birth and death of meaning* (2nd ed.). New York: Free Press.

Becker, E. (1973). *The denial of death*. New York: Free Press.

Berry, J. W. (1969). On cross-cultural comparability. *International Journal of Psychology, 4*, 119–128.

Jonas, E., & Fritsche, I. (2013). Destined to die but not to wage war: How existential threat can contribute to escalation or de-escalation of violent intergroup conflict. *American Psychologist, 68*, 543–558.

Kluckhohn, F. (1950). Dominant and substitute profiles of cultural orientations: Their significance for the analysis of social stratification. *Social Forces, 28*, 376–393.

Kluckhohn, C. (1954). Southwestern studies of culture and personality. *American Anthropologist, 56*(4), 685–697.

Kluckhohn, C. (1956). Culture and behavior. In G. Lindsey (Ed.), *Handbook of social psychology* (Vol. II, pp. 921–976). Redding, MA: Addison-Wesley.

Lee, D. (1950). Lineal and nonlineal codifications of reality. *ETC: A Review of General Semantics, 8*(1), 13–26.

Lonner, W. J. (2000). Revisiting the search for psychological universals. *Cross-Cultural Psychology Bulletin, 34*(1–2), 34–37.

Maslow, A. H. (1954). The instinctoid nature of basic needs. *Journal of Personality, 22*(3), 326–347.

Maslow, A. H. (1987). *Motivation and personality (revised by R. Frager, J. Fadiman, C. McReynolds, & R. Cox)*. New York: Harper & Row.

Napoleon, H. (1996). *Yuuyaraq: The way of the human being*. Fairbanks, AK: University of Alaska Fairbanks, Native Knowledge Network.

Pettigrew, T. F. (1998). Intergroup contact theory. *Annual Review of Psychology, 49*(1), 65–85.

Pike, K. (1967). *Language in relation to a unified theory of the structure of human behavior*. The Hague, NL: Erlbaum.

Pyszczynski, T., Greenberg, J., & Koole, S. L. (2004). Experimental existential psychology: Exploring the human confrontation with reality. In J. Greenberg, S. L. Koole, & T. Pyszczynski (Eds.), *Handbook of experimental existential psychology* (pp. 3–12). New York: Guilford.

Salzman, M. (2001). Cultural trauma and recovery: Perspectives from terror management theory. *Trauma, Violence & Abuse, 2*(2), 172–191.

Salzman, M. (2005). The dynamics of cultural trauma: Implications for the pacific nations. In A. J. Marsella, A. Austin, & B. Grant (Eds.), *Social change and psychosocial adaptation in the Pacific Islands: Cultures in transition* (pp. 29–52). New York: Springer.

Salzman, M. (2012). Dehumanization as a prerequisite of atrocity and killing. In D. J. Christie & J. E. Pim (Eds.), *Nonkilling psychology* (pp. 107–124). Honolulu, HI: Global Center for Non-Killing.

Sherif, M., Harvey, O. J., White, B. J., Hood, W. R., & Sherif, C. W. (1954/1961). *Social judgment*. New Haven, CT: Yale University Press.

Smith, P. B., Fischer, R., Vignoles, V. L., & Bond, M. H. (2013). *Understanding social psychology across cultures: Engaging with others in a changing world* (2nd ed.). London: Sage.

Snyder, M., & Miene, P. (1994). On the functions of stereotypes and prejudice. In *The psychology of prejudice: The Ontario symposium* (Vol. 7, pp. 33–54). Hillsdale, NJ: Lawrence Erlbaum.

Solomon, S., Greenberg, J., & Pyszczynski, T. (2004). The cultural animal: Twenty years of terror management theory and research. In J. Greenberg & S. L. K. Pyszczynski (Eds.), *Handbook of experimental existential psychology* (pp. 13–34). New York: Guilford.

Triandis, H. C., Chan, D. K.-S., Bhawuk, D. P. S., Iwao, S., & Sinha, J. B. P. (1995). Multimethod probes of allocentrism and idiocentrism. *International Journal of Psychology, 30*, 461–480.

Triandis, H. C., & Gelfand, M. (2012). A theory of individualism and collectivism. In P. A. M. Van Lange, A. W. Kruglanski, & E. T. Higgins (Eds.), *Handbook of social psychological theories* (Vol. 2, pp. 498–520). Los Angeles, CA: Sage.

Yalom, I. (1980). *Existential psychotherapy*. New York: Basic Books.

Zimbardo, P. (2007). *The Lucifer effect: Understanding how good people turn evil*. New York: Random House.

Chapter 3
Culture and Human Needs

Core Human Needs and Concerns: What do humans really need and why?
Physiological needs
Psychological needs
Existential needs
Culture as an ontological prescription of how to "be" and "how to live."
Culture as a "road map for living"
Culture and "Doing the right thing"

3.1 Culture and Human Needs: What Do Anxiety-Prone Human Creatures Really Need?

In seeking bedrock this volume looks to the human condition. Embedded in the human condition are real needs that motivate humans to act in the pursuit of satisfying those needs. Human needs are both physiological and psychological. They are an essential aspect of the human condition and we are challenged to address these existential realities. These needs and core concerns are assumed to be universal while how people address those needs varies across cultures. What do humans really need and how do cultures respond to these core human needs and concerns? What human needs are addressed by culture? What are the consequences of traumatic cultural disruption? Why and how do cultures change in response to environmental and ecological demands?

3.2 Physiological Needs and Cultures

The first requirement of life is to live. In order for a people to survive they must adapt to the ecological realities that contextualize their lives. As noted (Triandis & Gelfand, 2012) ecological correlates of cultural differences such as the consequences of relative abundance or scarcity of resources affect attitudes towards

M.B. Salzman, *A Psychology of Culture*, International and Cultural Psychology,
https://doi.org/10.1007/978-3-319-69420-7_3

perceived in-groups and out-groups. They note that when resources are abundant there is a greater tendency towards individualism and looseness (loose adherence to norms) whereas when resources are scarce and cultures are relatively isolated from other cultures people are required to work cooperatively with each other while under the behavioral requirements of strict norms often rigorously enforced.

There is an association of ecology and culture regarding the constructs of individualism and collectivism. For example, collectivism most frequently occurs in agricultural societies. Rural samples are more collectivist than urban samples. There is a demonstrable association of ecology and culture regarding these constructs. In agricultural cultures, for example cooperation may be necessary for survival (Triandis, 1994) because it is required to fulfill the demands of physiological survival. As a result, socialization and child rearing practices emphasize the development of qualities such as dependability, responsibility, and conformity (p. 23). In contrast, in ecologies where survival depends on hunting and gathering where physical mobility, independent thought, and self reliance is needed to track and find prey, and gather necessities the child rearing practices reflect this ecological requirement. Triandis (1994) offers an interesting association between ecological conditions and cultural responses to those conditions that serve an adaptive function. He describes an ecological context where an infestation of tsetse flies decimated herds of cattle leading to a scarcity of milk. Adaptive responses to this scarcity "such as polygamy, postpartum sex taboos, sleeping arrangements, close mother son relations in early life, initiation ceremonies and more distant relationships in later life (p. 23)." Responses to industrialization, urbanization, globalization and technological innovation influence child rearing practices, family structure and educational policy. Thus, the realities of an ecological environment create the conditions for the development and transmission of particular cultural responses. When the ecological demands of survival change cultures respond more or less successfully.

3.3 Culture and Psychological Needs

Maslow (1968, p. 206) thought that "The human needs a framework of values, a philosophy of life …in about the same sense that he needs sunlight, calcium, and love." Frankl, V.E. (1946/1984) asserted that "There is nothing in the world …that would so effectively help one to survive even the worst conditions as the knowledge that there is meaning in one's life." The human experience of meaning in life is thought to be a foundation of wellbeing and is in fact a central human motivation. Heintzelman and King (2014), in their review of relevant literature, cite self-report research indicating that a sense of meaning in ones' life is associated with higher quality of life, superior self-reported health and even decreased mortality. Furthermore, a sense of meaning in life has been associated with lower incidence of psychological disorders (Mascaro & Rosen, 2005) and suicidal ideation. Meaning in life has also been positively associated with such factors as heightened occupational adjustment and greater use of adaptive coping strategies (Thompson, Coker, Krause, & Henry, 2003).

If, as many suggest, self-esteem is a vital psychological resource and human need how, then, is self-esteem constructed? Can self-esteem be constructed in a world and life perceived as meaningless? The perspective of this book strongly endorses the view that meaning is a human need and this need is addressed by culture. But what is "meaning" and "meaningfulness?" There are numerous perspectives. Broadly considered meaning may be conceived of as a set of mental representations of the expected relationships or associations connecting people, places, objects and beliefs to each other (e.g., Baumeister, 1991; McGregor & Little, 1998). This conceptualization includes many related concepts such as worldviews, "folk" psychologies (Bruner, 1990), system relevant ideologies (Jost & Banajii, 1994) and others. Most importantly for this examination, meaning serves as a lens through which people view and interpret the world and provides guidelines for how people should behave in varied situations. It helps people cope with traumatic life events (e.g., Frankl, 1946) and manage the "terror inherent in the human condition" (existential terror). Thus meaning provides people with expectations for themselves, others and the world around them. It provides a "roadmap for living" and most importantly it provides for the opportunity to construct the self perception that one has value in a meaningful world resulting in what we call self-esteem. Maintaining a sense of meaning has been proposed as a fundamental human need (Dik et al., 2003). The perspective of this book supports this proposition and all that follows including the assertion that humans are motivated to meet their needs, as they perceive them through whatever pathways and means perceived as available to them. Perhaps our task is to develop communities and social systems that offer many accessible and multiple pathways to constructive self-esteem.

The perspective and point of view taken in this book addresses these issues. Human needs as described below are proposed as universal. How those needs are addressed varies across cultures in response to the ecology and environment to which it responds. A founder of humanistic psychology, Abraham Maslow (1943, 1954, 1968), provides a useful point of departure for the consideration of those questions. What are truly universal (etic), culture specific (emic) and idiosyncratic (unique) aspects of our humanity. As we see below Maslow considered self-esteem to be a universal need. It is, however, constructed differently across cultures. How should we be (personality characteristics), how should we act with fellow humans? What goals should we strive for? These are core questions we all must address in order to achieve the conviction that one has value in a meaningful world. Maslow's original formulation of his theory proposed that humans are motivated to address and satisfy their real needs. He proposed the following human needs that motivate our behavior. The earliest and most widespread version of Maslow's (1943, 1954) *hierarchy of needs* includes five motivational needs, often depicted as hierarchical levels within a pyramid. What is universal (etic) and what is culture specific (emic)? The point of view of this book is that human needs are universal. The motivation of humans to meet their essential needs is universal but how humans strive to satisfy these needs varies across cultures and varies idiosyncratically. What do humans really need?

- Biological and Physiological needs—air, food, drink, shelter, warmth, sex, sleep.
- Safety needs—protection from elements, security, order, law, limits, and stability.

- Social needs—Belongingness and Love—work group, family, affection, relationships.
- Esteem needs—self-esteem, achievement, mastery, status, and respect.
- Self-Actualization needs—realizing personal potential, self-fulfillment, seeking personal growth and peak experiences.

This original and most widely known five-stage model can be divided into basic (or deficiency) needs (e.g. physiological, safety, love, and esteem) and growth needs (self-actualization). He proposed that lower order needs (i.e., food, water, air) must be satisfied before higher order needs (i.e., self actualization) can be successfully addressed and achieved. It is noteworthy that Maslow's (1943, 1954) five stage model has been expanded to include cognitive and aesthetic needs (Maslow, 1970a) and later transcendence needs (Maslow, 1970b).

Maslow thought that humans need self-esteem. Why? TMT researchers and theorists note that self-esteem is inversely related to anxiety (see Greenberg et al., 1997). Anxiety is an aversive state that humans seek relief from by various means. It is, due to our sophisticated cognitive capacity to reflect on self and the future, a part of the human condition. Bolstering self-esteem reduces anxiety and self-esteem may be constructed differently across cultures and sought in constructive, positive, mistaken or destructive ways (i.e., bullying). Self-esteem, as discussed by Becker (1971) and TMT theorists saw self-esteem as that warm feeling of being of value in a meaningful universe. Frankl (1968), from his perspective as a Holocaust survivor proposed a system of psychotherapy designed to construct or reconstruct a world of meaning. He wrote, "It is one of the basic tenets of logotherapy that man's main concern is not to gain pleasure or to avoid pain, but rather to see a meaning in his life" (p. 179). If meaning is essential for the construction of anxiety-buffering self-esteem one may see that culture infuses the world with meaning.

Yalom (1980) considered four basic conflicts that emerge from the human's confrontation with the givens of existence. These givens that are assumed to be universally inherent in the human condition are "ultimate concerns." He identified these as *death, freedom and responsibility, existential isolation, and meaninglessness.* Physical death, an undeniable human universal and our awareness of it, is an obvious concern. This awareness presents humans with an existential problem. Yalom thought that that the awareness of our mortality is a core existential conflict. It is a conflict between the awareness of the inevitability of our physical annihilation and our drive to continue to be. The concerns of freedom and responsibility and existential isolation Yalom identified may be more prominent in western cultures but the concern with the existence and construction of meaning seems to be inherent in the human condition. Questions such as why we exist, what is the meaning of life, what is the meaning and purpose of *my* life are questions that arise early in life and persists throughout it. The possibility that there is no inherent meaning in life other than what we create is, to say the least, disconcerting as we seem to seek greater certainty through social consensus and validation to support our belief in a world of meaning within which anxiety prone humans may be guided to a life of significance and personal value.

Self–Determination Theory (SDT), takes a different perspective and proposes that certain evolved psychological needs must be satisfied if individuals are to achieve and develop to their fullest potential (Deci & Ryan, 2000). SDT proposes three universal needs: autonomy, competence, and relatedness. Autonomy here is conceived a perceiving one's behavior as freely chosen and volitional rather than imposed by external forces. Relatedness involves the need to feel a sense of connectedness and belonging. Competence is the need to feel that one's is capable and effective in one's actions. STD researchers and theorists also propose that these are universal needs but their expression and means of satisfying these needs vary across cultures. The proposed need for autonomy for example may be satisfied in collectivist cultures as behaving in ways consistent with group norms might be internalized as freely chosen or volitional.

Hood, Hill, and Williamson (2005) assert that the first basic question is "what do humans need (p. 12)." They provide an answer that is consistent with a central focus of this book, "Beyond the basic needs dictated by our biological requirements like air, food, shelter humans need and seek meaning. Religion is a meaning system (p. 12)." Culture is a meaning system. We need a world of meaning to act in order to achieve a sense of value and significance. There is evidence to support this proposition. The experience of living what is construed as a meaningful life is associated with a range of positive effects and outcomes (Heintzelman & King, 2014). People seek, construct and need meaning.

In fact, self-report data indicates that the perception of living a meaningful life seems to promote a host of benefits for the human organism (Heintzelman & King, 2014) such as slower rates of age related cognitive decline, lower incidence of psychological disorders and suicide ideation (Steger & Kashdan, 2009). Those who report that their lives are meaningful report greater reliance on effective coping strategies and heightened occupational adjustment. People who report that their lives are meaningful are even rated as more socially appealing (Stillman, Lambert, Fincham, & Baumeister, 2011).

The relevance of meaningfulness and psychological well-being was explored by Volgert, Schulz, Levke-Bruitt, and Andreas (2013). They focused on the relationship of meaningfulness to clinical diagnosis and psychotherapy outcomes. Their study investigated 314 inpatients with mental disorders and 856 "healthy" control subjects using self-report measures of meaning in life (MiL). They found that patients showed lower MiL compared to controls and also found diagnostic specific differences in MiL for depression and that MiL increased in the course of treatment and remained stable at follow-up. They concluded that there was evidence that for lower MiL in inpatients with a spectrum of mental disorders. This was especially true for patients with depression compared to controls. Furthermore, perceived meaning improves over the course of psychotherapy. They conclude that meaning construction in therapy may be useful to help patients overcome psychological problems and make life worth living. It would seem that meaning in life has important clinical implications for the support of mental health and psychological well-being. Frankl (1968) and Yalom (1980) would certainly agree. This suggests that perception of meaningfulness in life and the world is a human need as well as the prerequisite for the construction of the belief that one is of value (self-esteem) in a meaningful world.

Frankl (1968) wrote that "man's (sic) main concern is not to gain pleasure or to avoid pain, but rather to see a meaning in his life." p. 179. According to his logotherapy "the striving to find meaning in life is the primary motivational force in man (p. 154)." He noted that humans are "able to live and die for the sake of ideals and values" (p. 155). There are, of course different perspectives and aspects of meaning, a meaningful life and a meaningful world to act in. These perspectives seem to converge on the notion that the world one inhabits *makes sense*. That is, a sense of *what is,* and why *that is.* This includes a sense of *purpose* in a meaningful and coherent world. Cultures and religions describe such a world and how one should act in it (Proulx, Markman, & Lindberg, 2013; Solomon, Greenberg, & Pyszcyznski, 1991). The classical Hindu text, for example, the Bhagavad-Gita (Easwaran, 2007) teaches that it is through our relationship with the whole that is the source of meaning. It teaches that everything has a place in the universe and people have duties to perform within that role. It suggests that we should act and think in consciousness of our role in the larger wholes in which we are a part: our families, organizations and ultimately our sacred universe. This universe is, according to its teaching, divine and the locus of meaning. When Krishna revealed himself to be the universe and identical to its divinity we can see that our individual actions are connected to the cosmos as a whole and therefore to divinity as we are a part of that divine universe. Thus meaning is infused in all of our actions, thoughts and the words we speak. The Bhagavad-Gita, then, describes a worldview subscribed to by millions. Within that worldview are prescriptions indicating how to BE and how to ACT. The teachings prescribe action characterized by discipline and detachment that are firm in discipline and not attached to its ephemeral consequences or concerned with success or failure.

From the perspective of the Individual Psychology of Alfred Adler the striving for "significance" is a central motivation as a compensatory striving to overcome feelings of inferiority that he deemed to be universal (Ansbacher & Ansbacher, 1946). These feelings of inferiority are rooted in the earliest of human experience as a helpless and dependent infant whose infancy extends for a relatively long time. It is also rooted in the existential and cosmic awareness of our smallness, vulnerability and mortality in an awesome and terrifying universe. How and what a person chooses to strive for significance represents the individual's psychological movement through life. Adler referred to this as a persons' style of life. This is the self-esteem motive that is considered to be universal though culturally and individually expressed and constructed. Kruglanski et al. (2013) proposed that a "quest for significance" motivated acts of terrorism where the goal of the behavior is the achievement, defense, or recovery of significance. It is the sense that one is indeed "somebody," that one matters in this life and world. It is the general motivating force beyond simply survival. The significance quest is the "attainment of what the culture says is worth attaining" (p. 561). One may question Maslow's assumption that lower order needs (i.e., biological, survival) must be satisfied before higher order needs can be achieved is questionable when considering the behavior of the suicide bomber who internalized cultural norms and values that suggest a transcendent heroism following death by "martyrdom." In some cases, it seems that the self-esteem needs (the quest for significance) overwhelm the basic biological motive to continue existence. Our goals and the means we choose to achieve them are grounded in the norms and values offered by culture(s) that may be wholly or selectively internalized and sampled by anxiety prone humans. What happens when a culturally based system of meaning is traumatically disrupted by apparently inexplicably disaster?

3.4 Culture as a Roadmap for Living

Culture has been defined as a system of shared meanings. If meaning is a human need then the disruption of culture(s) should, predictively have serious consequences as need deprivation is an aversive state. In fact, cultural disintegration and dislocation have been associated with certain patterns of personal and social dysfunction such as substance abuse, hopelessness and suicide. In order to comprehend and address these expressions of human suffering it is necessary to consider essential psychological functions of culture, predictable consequences of traumatic cultural disruption and implications for recovery. Such consequences are common across genetically and geographically diverse indigenous peoples as Alaska Natives, Native Hawaiians, Australian aboriginals and others whose cultures have been assaulted and disrupted as a result of contact and colonization with Western powers. One example is illustrated by a suicide epidemic that has afflicted the Guarani Indians of the western Brazilian state of Mato Grosso do Sul as reported by Lyons (2015) in the New York Times "Week in Review" (p. 6). He reports that indigenous peoples suffer the greatest risk of suicide than any ethnic or cultural groups in the world. Given the geographical and genetic variation among these afflicted people one must seek other explanations for this plague. This observable fact may be attributed to common experiences where tribe members have seen the upheaval of their culture that produces a lack of confidence, meaning and grounding about who they are, how to be and how to live. This reality has ignited cultural recovery movements among indigenous peoples across vast geographical and genetic variation. There are many such examples of culturally traumatized (Salzman, 2001) indigenous peoples across the globe. The worldwide voyage of the Hokule'a and Hikianalia, reconstructed traditional style Polynesian voyaging canoes, are an impetus and example of the cultural renaissance evident in Hawai'i. Currently on a world-wide voyage using traditional navigational techniques such as star navigation to traverse the oceans retracing the voyages of ancient Polynesians as they explore and settled. These voyages fueled a resurrection of traditional values and meaning such as "malama honua (caring for the earth)." The first of these voyages was to Tahiti in 1976 and a cultural renaissance and sovereignty movement were and are being fueled by the power of these meaningful reconnections not only in Hawai'i but throughout the Polynesian Pacific. A report in the Honolulu Star Advertiser (Zunin, Honolulu Star Advertiser, 2014) suggests that in the Marquesas traditional life is coming back from "the brink of extinction." The report indicates that "of all the Polynesian island groups, The Marquesas suffered the greatest population decline from diseases brought by Western contact" (p. B6). What may account for the motive to reconstruct cultures among peoples whose traditional cultures have been traumatically disrupted?

So we must consider the psychological functions and role of cultures in addressing core human needs such as a sense of coherence, purpose, value and its source that is, meaning.

3.5 Cultural Prescriptions for Being and *Doing the Right Thing*

Culture offers ontological prescriptions of how to "be" and "how to live." The question is universal and the answers vary according to specific circumstances and ecological realities. In this sense cultures offer a "road map for living" and a moral universe that tells us how to do the right thing. The idea of culture as a roadmap for living was expressed by a Native American elder at the conclusion of the 1998 Congress of the International Association for Cross-Cultural Psychology that the author attended and participated in. After days of brilliant, sophisticated, detailed, and somewhat reductionist presentations analyzing the various aspects of culture this elegant definition of culture struck the author as exactly right. She said, "My culture is my road map for living." I looked to various foundational world cultures for roadmaps and the explicit or implicit worldviews they emerged from.

In the rich tradition of Buddhism we may find a description of the universe, life and prescriptions defining how to live a meaningful and life. A Buddhist worldview proposes "Four Noble Truths" that describe life and how to deal with it. It posits that:

- To live is to suffer: There are many forms of suffering including unease, physical or psychological pain, illness, and bereavement.
- Attachment is the cause of suffering.
- There can be an end to suffering.
- There is a path to end suffering. The Eightfold Path.

A description of how to live without suffering is offered if one lives correctly. The Noble Eightfold Path is the path it is described as the middle way of neither asceticism nor hedonism. The Noble Eightfold Path describes eight steps to enlightenment. Enlightenment was the Buddha's quest and accomplishment (Nasrasu

1993) and the spiritual goal of believers in this system. The path defines the way to live and how to be in this life. It seems explicit. It tells adherents how to *Do the Right Thing.*

- Right View
- Right Resolve
- Right Speech
- Right Action
- Right Livelihood
- Right Effort
- Right Mindfulness
- Right Concentration

The eightfold path's prescription of "right action," for example is explicit. For example:

- Buddhists strive to do nothing that could harm other living beings
- Practice of the defined virtues such as unselfishness, kindness, benevolence, compassion, charity, and generosity. These should be cultivated and practiced in one's life.

These are virtues derived from the eightfold path that indicate how to *be.* These are virtues to be cultivated and practiced by adherents through the eightfold path in order to advance the individual in the moral universe of the belief system.

So, as proposed, culture(s) provide just those rules and customs, goals of conduct that place "right actions" and "right ways of being" at the person's disposal. Is this a need of anxiety prone human creatures as we confront life in a wondrous and terrifying existence?

Other systems, perhaps all worldviews, also address the foundational existential questions addressed by culture. In Jewish tradition as described by Rabbi Telushkin (1994, p. 33) in his compendium of "Jewish Wisdom" offered a description and prescription of how to be a good person and or a "Mensch" in a moral and meaningful universe. In addition to the universal or near universal Golden Rule of "Love your neighbor as yourself" and its equivalents such expressions as "Do not do unto others what is hateful to yourself" he offers these:

- "The Torah hold Jews to a standard of what is right and good" not "what is profitable."
- "Do not stand by while your neighbor's blood is shed." (Leviticus 19:16)
- "So follow the way of the good, and keep to the paths of the just" (Proverbs 2:20)
- "You shall be holy…" it's not enough to NOT DO what is prohibited to be a good person (Leviticus 19.2)
- Justice, justice you shall pursue (Deuteronomy) 16:20

The author was socialized in Jewish culture and internalized some but not all of its prescriptions for being a good person in a meaningful world. He has internalized what Einstein proposed as the core of what it means to be Jewish or should be are the values of:

- the pursuit of knowledge for its own sake
- the pursuit for social justice

When the author perceives himself as working for justice and pursuing knowledge he feels little anxiety and much meaning. Such examples may be construed as a "Roadmap for Living." Do we need a roadmap to guide us in *how to live* and indeed *why to live*?

Confucianism is another example of the prescriptive function of culture that addresses the core human questions of *how to be* and *how to live and act* in other words it provides a *roadmap for living* for anxiety prone human creatures. *Di zi jui*, a guide for youth and families based on Confucianist principles, offers just such prescriptive guidance (Wenzhong, 2010). It prescribes, for example, how children should behave at home and how students should act in school. It advises youth to be dutiful at home, to listen respectfully to parents, be dutiful to one's parents maintain a disciplined life and strive for good results in one's studies. If there is a less than optimum results in school, the solution is to increase effort. If failure in school is attributed to a lack of sufficient effort, then there is a remedy and that is to work harder. This attribution of failure seems far more conducive to success than attributing failure to a presumed "learning disability" or deficiency.

The prescriptive function of culture as a *roadmap for living* is further evidenced by its standards for siblings as described by *Di zi jui* (Wenzhong, 2010). When seniors are away from home older siblings are advised to befriend the younger ones. Younger siblings are advised to respect and love the older ones. These behavioral prescriptions serve to support and maintain harmonious relationships and harmony in the family and society, which is a high Confucianist value. Finally, the teaching advises that after these and other guidelines are accomplished one should study further and improve one's cultural and spiritual life. Confucianism is and has been, a powerful cultural force that exerts great influence in the world. It is a clear example of the prescriptive function of culture in providing a *roadmap for living* for those who accept the worldview and seek answers to the fundamental human question of *how to be* and *what to do*. The answers to these questions that are embedded in the human condition are of compelling concern to anxiety-prone human creatures. Cultures address these questions.

3.6 Personal Note

The author worked with Alaska Natives in a human services program in the early 1990s where cultural values were implemented throughout the program. Stories, place names and traditional ceremonies were revived and emphasized in a process of what appeared to the author to be an effort at cultural reconstruction after the traumatic effects of contact with colonizers. The revival was fueled by a series of Elder conferences held around the state during the 1980s as Elders and communities became alarmed at the level of psychological and behavioral distress that were undeniable. The Inupiat Ilitqusiat program designed to guide the Iñupiat people (an Alaska

Native people) in how to BE an Iñupiat that translates as how to be the real people. Ilitqusiat that translates as that which makes us who we are. The question of how to BE is a core existential concern and question that is addressed by cultures. This philosophy was developed over thousands of years and articulated by the Elders as part of the Spirit Movement of the 1980s (Greenback, 1996). The movement got started in the early 80s because there was serious concern that young people were being exposed to unhealthy lifestyles as a result of poor role modeling. Elder's saw that young people were turning to alcohol, drugs and suicide. Elders were concerned that cultural values were not being transmitted across generations. Elder's conferences identified core cultural values to guide people how to be an Iñupiat or real person or how to be a human being. They advise that every "Iñupiaq person is responsible to all other Iñupiat for the survival of our cultural spirit and the values and traditions through which it survives. Through our extended family, we retain, teach and live our Iñupiaq way of life. With guidance and support from our Elders, we teach our children our Iñupiat Ilitqusiat values." They identified the following core values:

- Knowledge of Family Tree
- Love of Children
- Avoid Conflict
- Knowledge of Language
- Cooperation
- Family Roles

This process and its product are examples of cultural responses to the universal existential concern of HOW TO BE and HOW TO ACT in this existence and world. It represents a "roadmap for living." Do we, anxiety prone human beings, need a "roadmap for living?" Do we need a world of meaning to act in? How is meaning constructed?

References

Ansbacher, H., & Ansbacher, R. (1946). *The individual psychology of Alfred Adler*. New York: Basic Books.

Baumeister, R. F. (1991). *Meanings of life*. New York: Guilford Press.

Becker, E. (1971). *The birth and death of meaning* (2nd ed.). New York: Free Press.

Bruner, J. (1990). Culture and human development: A new look. *Human Development, 33*(6), 344–355.

Deci, E. L., & Ryan, R. M. (2000). The "what" and "why" of goal pursuits: Human needs and the self-determination of behavior. *Psychological Inquiry, 11*(4), 227–268.

Dik, B. J., Steger, M. F., Fitch-Martin, A. R., & Onder, C. C. (2013). Cultivating meaningfulness at work. In *The experience of meaning in life* (pp. 363-377). Springer, Dordrecht.

Easwaran, E. (2007). *Trans. The Bhagavad Gita*. New Delhi: Nilgiri Press.

Frankl, V. E. (1946). *Man's searching for meaning. Preface to 1984 edition.*

Frankl, V. E. (1968). *Man's search for meaning: An introduction to logotherapy*. New York: Washington Square Press.

Greenback, F. (1996). *The Inupiat ilitqusiat program.* AK: Village News Network.

Greenberg, J., Solomon, S., & Pyszczynski, T. (1997). Terror management theory of self-esteem and cultural worldviews: Empirical assessments and conceptual refinements. *Advances in Experimental Social Psychology, 29*, 61–139.

Heintzelman, S. J., & King, L. A. (2014). Life is pretty meaningful. *American Psychologist, 69*(6), 561–574. https://doi.org/10.1037/a0035049.

Hood, R. W., Hill, P. C., & Williamson, W. P. (2005). *The psychology of religious fundamentalism*. New York: Guilford.

Jost, J. T., & Banaji, M. R. (1994). The role of stereotyping in system-justification and the production of false consciousness. *British Journal of Social Psychology, 33*(1), 1–27.

Kruglanski, A. W., Belanger, J. J., Gelfand, M., Gunarantna, R., Hettiarachchi, M., Reinares, F., Orehek, E., Sosata, J., & Sharvit, K. (2013). Terrorism—A (self) love story: Redirecting the significance quest can end violence. *American Psychologist, 68*, 559–575. https://doi.org/10.1037/a0032615.

Lyons, C. (2015, January 4). Suicides spreads through a Brazilian tribe. *The New York Times, Sunday Review*, p. 6.

Maslow, A. H. (1943). A theory of human motivation. *Psychological Review, 50*(4), 370–396.

Maslow, A. H. (1954). *Motivation and personality*. New York: Harper and Row.

Maslow, A. H. (1968). *Toward a psychology of being*. New York: D. Van Nostrand.

Maslow, A. H. (1970a). *Motivation and personality*. New York: Harper & Row.

Maslow, A. H. (1970b). *Religions, values, and peak experiences*. New York: Penguin. (Original work published 1964).

Mascaro, N., & Rosen, D. H. (2005). Existential meaning's role in the enhancement of hope and prevention of depressive symptoms. *Journal of Personality, 73*(4), 985–1014.

McGregor, I., & Little, B. R. (1998). Personal projects, happiness, and meaning: On doing well and being yourself. *Journal of Personality and Social Psychology, 74*(2), 494.

Nasrasu, P. L. (1993). *The essence of Buddhism*. New Delhi: Asian Educational Services.

Proulx, T., Markman, K. D., & Lindberg, M. J. (2013). The new science of meaning. In K. D. Markman, T. Proulx, & M. J. Lindberg (Eds.), *The psychology of meaning* (pp. 3–14). Washington, DC: American Psychological Association. https://doi.org/10.1037/14040-000.

Salzman, M. B. (2001). Cultural trauma and recovery: Perspectives from terror management theory. *Trauma, Violence, & Abuse, 2*(2), 172–191.

Solomon, S., Greenberg, J., & Pyszcyznski, T. (1991). A terror management theory of social behavior: The psychological functions of self-esteem and cultural worldviews. In M. P. Zanna (Ed.), *Advances in experimental social psychology* (pp. 91–159). San Diego: Academic Press.

Steger, M. F., & Kashdan, T. B. (2009). Depression and everyday social activity, belonging, and well-being. *Journal of Counseling Psychology, 56*(2), 289.

Stillman, T. F., Baumeister, R. F., & Mele, A. R. (2011). Free will in everyday life: Autobiographical accounts of free and unfree actions. *Philosophical Psychology, 24*(3), 381–394.

Telushkin, J. (1994). *Jewish Wisdom*. Ethical. *Spiritual, and Historical Lessons from the Great Works and Thinkers*. New York: William Morrow.

Thompson, N. J., Coker, J., Krause, J. S., & Henry, E. (2003). Purpose in life as a mediator of adjustment after spinal cord injury. *Rehabilitation Psychology, 48*(2), 100.

Triandis, H. C. (1994). *Culture and social behavior*.

Triandis, H. C., & Gelfand, M. (2012). A theory of individualism and collectivism. In P. A. M. Van Lange, A. W. Kruglanski, & E. T. Higgins (Eds.), *Handbook of social psychological theories* (Vol. 2, pp. 498–520). Los Angeles, CA: Sage.

Volgert, J., Schulz, H., Levke-Bruitt, A., & Andreas, S. (2013). Meaning in life: Relationship to clinical diagnosis and psychotherapy outcome. *Journal of Clinical Psychology, 70*(6), 528–535. https://doi.org/10.1002/jclp.22053.

Wenzhong, Q. (2010). *Di zi gui*. Beijing: China Youth Press.

Yalom, I. (1980). *Existential psychotherapy*. New York: Basic Books.

Zunin, I. (2014, June 4). Cultural reawakening brings Marquesas back from the brink. *Honolulu Star Advertiser*, p. B6.

Chapter4
Culture and Self-Esteem

The self-esteem motive
The anxiety buffering effects of self-esteem.
Social Identity
The human need for meaning

What do human beings really need? Can we prevent human problems by addressing real human needs? Do cultures address human needs?

Maslow (1968), as indicated previously, proposed a hierarchy of human needs that included the need to feel a sense of belonging and self-esteem as well as basic physiological needs (air, food, water, etc.), safety and "self-actualization." He suggested that the higher order psychological needs (e.g., self-esteem and self-actualization) could not be realized until the lower order needs (physiological, safety and belonging) are satisfied. This assertion may be only partly valid as, for example, safety needs may be compromised when "belonging needs" are unfulfilled as the individual likely feels safer when one feels connected to others and experiences a real sense of belonging to something larger than self. Becker (1971, 1973) and the empirically tested Terror Management Theory (Greenberg, Solomon, & Pyszczynski, 1997) he inspired indicate that self-esteem is a vital psychological resource that provides a powerful motivation of human behavior may well be the dominant human motive. Terror management theory (TMT) suggests that the power of this motive is related to its anxiety buffering characteristics. Some have maintained that self-esteem is a Western "emic" but this perspective indicates that it is a universal need that is constructed differently across cultures. It is, therefore, a cultural construction. Self-esteem can only be constructed in a meaningful world. In a world absent of meaning how can a sense of value be cultivated? Culture and religion infuse the world with meaning. They describe a coherent version of reality (cultural worldview) that may explain life, the nature of reality, and the meaning of one's experience. Cultural worldviews vary widely but all seem to offer (Solomon, Greenberg, & Pyszczynski, 1991):

M.B. Salzman, *A Psychology of Culture*, International and Cultural Psychology,
https://doi.org/10.1007/978-3-319-69420-7_4

- A description of how the world was created
- Prescriptions for what for what people should to live a good life and to be of value in a meaningful world
- Some promise of immortality literal (as in eternal life) or symbolic by contributing to something larger that self that continues past one's mortal life (as in the nation and its symbols)
- What kind of persons we should strive to be to achieve value in a culturally prescribed (and internalized) world of meaning?

Shweder (1991) as noted earlier proposed that due to the principle of existential uncertainty humans are, from birth, motivated to extrapolate meanings from the events, situations, and environments with which we interact.

Baumeister (1991) identified four overlapping needs for meaning. The need for meaning includes the need for purpose (seeing one's life as oriented toward some imagined goal or state); value (seeing one's actions as right or justifiable); efficacy (having a sense of control over events); self-worth (seeing one's life as having positive value). Culture infuses the world with meaning. It provides a canonical set of images, themes, values, plots and characters from which people may draw on to fashion their own unique stories including a constructed past, an experienced present and an imagined future (McAdams, 2013).

Self-esteem can only be achieved in a world of meaning. Maslow considered self-esteem to be a universal need. Indeed, Becker (1971) following Adler (see Ansbacher & Ansbacher, 1946) saw self-esteem as the dominant human motive as evidenced by the observation that when one is lacking this quality "they cannot act, they break down" (p. 75). Self-esteem is, however, constructed differently across cultures. How should we *be* (personality characteristics), how should we act (behavioral prescriptions) with my fellow humans in ways that bring positive outcomes and avoid danger? What goals should we strive for and how should we strive for them? What has value? Culture provides "just those rules and customs, goals of conduct that place right action (Becker, 1971, p. 79)" at the individuals' disposal. This is important when considering the central role of anxiety in the human condition.

4.1 Culture as a Psychological Defense

Becker proposed and TMT researchers have found that self-esteem serves as an essential anxiety buffering function that allows for the possibility of adaptive action. A principle and well-tested hypothesis of TMT (the anxiety buffer hypothesis) states that if a psychological structure provides protection against anxiety, then augmenting that structure should reduce anxiety in response to subsequent threats. Specifically, since self-esteem serves as a buffer against anxiety then strengthening self-esteem would be expected to reduce anxiety and anxiety-related behavior in response to threat (mortality salience). This hypothesis has been well supported empirically (see Greenberg et al., 1997 for review). Researchers (i.e., Schimel, Hayes, Williams, & Jahrig, 2007) have tested this hypothesis in varying ways. If anxiety-buffering self-esteem is constructed by a coherent worldview, then threat to that internalized world view should expose the subjects to anxiety. Since we are concerned with the anxiety resulting from our mortality and our awareness of our inability to fulfill the basic biological motive of continued existence the question of the relationship between threats to our internalized cultural worldviews and death-thought accessibility (DTA) bears scrutiny. Schimel et al. (2007) tested this hypothesis. Recall that according to TMT, if the cultural worldview protects people from thoughts about death, then weakening this structure should increase death-thought accessibility (DTA). These experimental social psychologists conducted five studies tested this DTA hypothesis. Study 1 showed that threatening Canadian participants' cultural values (vs. those of another culture) increased DTA on a word-fragment completion task. Study 2 showed that when participants could dismiss the threat, DTA remained low. Study 3 replicated the results of Study 1, but DTA was measured using a lexical decision task. Response latencies to death, negative, and neutral content were measured. Worldview threat increased DTA relative to accessibility for negative and neutral content. Study 4 showed that the DTA effect emerged independently of the arousal of anger or anxiety. Finally, Study 5 demonstrated that participants with a pro-creation (vs. pro-evolution) worldview had higher DTA after reading an anti-creation article.

The anxiety they refer to is the existential anxiety, rooted in the human condition that rumbles in the background of our conscious lives and that threatens to immobilize us if unmediated and un-buffered by the conviction that we have value in a meaningful world. The inverse relationship of self-esteem and anxiety is well established (see Solomon et al., 1991). This existential anxiety is the "terror" referred to in TMT. It is the result, as we shall explore, of a basic human problem. We are mortal and we know it. It is a universal fact that we face inevitable physical annihilation. What we believe about that fact and our conceptions of what follows varies across cultures. How do I *be* and what do I *do?* This is an essential existential question given our awareness of the reality that we cannot fulfill the basic biological motive that we share with all life that is, to continue existence. How do I function within this basic human problem?

4.2 Culture as a Roadmap for Living

Becker and TMT assert that culture provides just those rules, customs, and goals of conduct for the anxiety-prone human to allow for the construction of anxiety-buffering self-esteem. In this way culture serves to make continued self-esteem possible and provide the person with the conviction that s/he is of primary value in a world of meaningful action.

In the course ("A Psychology of Culture") that has inspired this book I recently gave students an assignment. I told them, following a screening of a film by the same name, to "Do the Right Thing." I asked them to note what that would be given the situations they encountered. I asked them to consider what the "Right Thing" was and where they may have derived that conviction. The prescription for a life and conduct with manageable anxiety (the "terror" rooted in the human condition) is to choose the "right" thing to do and the "right way" to be. Culture(s) offer guidance. Culture(s) offer a "roadmap for living."

These are core questions we all must address in order to achieve the conviction that one has value in a meaningful world, that one is "OK." Maslow's original formulation of his theory proposed that humans are motivated to address and satisfy their real needs. People need to feel that they matter, have value and are significant. Cultures show us the way. Cultures describe the world and cultures provide guidance in addressing the essential issues of how one should *be* in the world and what one should *do* in this world. As noted, cultures provide a description of the world and reality that many refer to as a "cultural worldview" and within the specific cultural worldview are behavioral and ontological prescriptions that if manifested and achieved allow may construct anxiety-buffering self-esteem to its adherents. What is the "right" way to be? What is the "right" thing to do? What if people differ on these essential questions? As we shall see humans face the common problems of existence across the globe but tend to answer these questions differently. Let's consider "answers" from some foundational world cultures.

4.3 Universal Human Problems and Varying Cultural Answers

Intercultural relations may be complicated by different answers and solutions to this and other common human problems. Kluckhohn (1950) identified six common human problems that cultures address in varying and often conflicting ways. These are:

- The relation of humans to nature
- What are the innate predispositions of humans?
- What are the types of personalities most valued?
- In what kind of space-time dimension does human action take place?
- How should we humans should relate to each other?
- What is the hierarchy of power in society and nature (and where do I fit in)?

These common human problems motivate varying answers and provide for the possibilities of multiple solutions to the problems of being human or perhaps these differences on such core concerns may lead to murderous conflict and intolerance. Cultures and religions address the crucial ontological questions of how to be and how to act in the world. We are motivated to address these needs.

The varying answers to such common human problems may also be a source of conflict between different meaning systems because of the centrality of these issues in the human condition. Cultures can be threatening to each other because they all ask and answer the same questions but the "answers" vary. All cultural world-views seem to offer a description of the world and how it was created, a prescription of what people should do and be in order to live good and meaningful lives and some hope of either literal (i.e., religiously inspired afterlife) or symbolic (i.e., culture, nation, "the American way") immortality. We feel, as McAdams (2013) suggested, anxiety when there is an absence of an answer to the question of "why?" He cites Camus's (1955) "Myth of Sisyphus" where the Gods punished Sisyphus by assigning him the pointless and meaningless task of pushing a large boulder up a hill only for it to roll down again. The gods apparently saw no greater torture than the "agony of pointlessness" (p. 6). In other words, an existence without a cogent answer to the question of "why" to explain and direct one's life is a source of profound existential anxiety and suffering. Only when Sisyphus could find meaning in his meaningless task could one imagine Sisyphus to be content.

4.4 Culture and Meaning

The existential perspective supported in this book suggests that life has no inherent meaning. Camus thought that an objective analysis of one's existence finds our existence to be "absurd (Camus, 1955)." For most, this is hardly a comforting thought. This existential perspective implies that we, universally, are born, we die and we make up everything in between. What we, collectively or individually "make up" includes culture. This thought suggests that all meaning in life is may be illusory (Heintzelman & King, 2014) and is rather unsettling given the potency and near sacred status of cultures because of the human needs they address. Illusions may serve positive or negative ends. Positive illusions are supportive of life, productive activity and hopefully make some contributions to adaptation and development. If meaning is constructed culturally and anxiety reducing self-esteem can only be constructed in a meaningful world, we can say that cultures infuse the world with meaning. Individuals may sample, emphasize and internalize specific aspects of one's culture, they can accept carte blanche one's culture of origin or weave together a world of meaning to act in from varied cultural sources. This perspective suggests that essential human questions that concern us all include whether or not our lives and what we do has purpose and that that purpose has value. These essential questions ask if what we do really matters and therefore imbuing our lives with significance in a meaningful world. Given our cognitive complexity and the ability to be aware of our mortality we need to feel that our lives matters in a way that will outlast our inevitable physical annihilation. We need to feel that the world is coherent and one's life makes sense. We need to know how *to be* and what *to do* in order to feel our lives matter, that we matter, that what we *do* and how we *be* has value, significance and adaptive utility in a meaningful world. Culture(s) infuse the world with meaning and are therefore serving an adaptive function through the construction of meaning.

Culture(s) provide answers to the question of "why" in that it organizes our existence and guides us in how we should live in that culture (s) provide "just those rules and customs, goals of conduct that place right action (Becker, 1971, p. 79)" at the individuals' disposal. Culture(s) also address the question of "what" in that it organizes our epistemic understanding of reality (McAdams, 2013). In other words, cultures provide a description of reality (cultural worldviews) and a roadmap for living within that worldview.

Becker (1975) thought that "culture itself is sacred, since it is the 'religion' that assures, in some way, the perpetuation of its members (p.4)" either literally or symbolically. In this sense culture embodies the transcendence of death in some form or another. Becker (1971) and others have concluded that virtually all cultures are fundamentally spiritual or religious in character. These belief systems and ideologies offer psychological sustenance in the form of a meaning system and, therefore, a foundation for the construction of essential self-esteem. Culture and religion infuse a persons' world with meaning and we are meaning seeking and meaning constructing organisms. Meaning help us navigate in a wondrous and terrifying existence in which we face the inevitability of physical annihilation that can occur at any time.

4.5 Culture as an Immortality Ideology

TMT proposes that these varying cultural worldviews serve, either literally or symbolically as an "immortality ideology." When different immortality ideologies collide the validity of each is called into question enhancing the possibility of psychological and behavioral defensive reactions that may result in distancing, demonization and attempts to convert "the other" to one's cultural or religious worldview or even the annihilation of those "others". Historical anti-Semitism provides an example of this dynamic. Goldhagen (1997) cited the religious roots of anti-Semitism by quoting John Chrysostom, "a pivotal church Father":

> Where Christ-killers gather, the cross is ridiculed, God blasphemed, the father unacknowledged, the son insulted, the grace of Spirit rejected...If the Jewish rites are holy and venerable, our way of life must be false. But if our way is true, as indeed it is, theirs is fraudulent. (p. 50)

Therefore, from this point of view, the worldview espoused by any given culture is a symbolic social construction that provides a meaningful context in which relatively anxiety free action is possible. Cognitively complex human beings are realistically concerned with their mortality and cultures address this concern. Therefore, culture addresses core human needs. How to deal with the observable fact that we face inevitable physical annihilation is a common human problem (etic) answered differently across cultures (emic) and immortality ideologies may clash on this vital concern. The anxiety driven need for absolute faith in one's worldview, given the high psychological stakes involved, can produce murderous reactions as well as serve to sustain people through their anxiety prone existence. A Beckerian (Becker, 1971, 1973) and TMT inspired conception of culture and its essential psychological functions expose some of the roots of such intolerance of cultural differences relating to core existential concerns. It seems that human differences on essential existential human concerns provide a context and tendency for intolerance. Which begs the question if must you be wrong for me to be right if we differ on this vital concern? Can we both be right? Can we both be wrong?

If humans need and strive for meaning in life its constituents bear examination. How is meaning in life constructed, maintained and reconstructed. In their review of relevant literature concerning the definitions and prevalence of meaning in life Heintzelman and King (2014) found three common themes. The first is that a meaningful life must have a sense of purpose. Secondly, a meaningful life is a life that has significance. The striving for significance is, then, a striving for meaning. Thirdly, a meaningful life makes sense to the person living it. When the world makes sense life seems more meaningful. The striving for significance and the search for meaning are central to the thinking of Adler and Frankl. Culture provides pathways to both. The achievement of a sense of meaning, whether culturally or religiously constructed provides us with the conviction that what one does has purpose and significance. The achievement of a sense of meaning may provide access to a perception that one's life matters in a way that will outlast one's physical existence. In this sense, the perception and belief that one's life is meaningful constitutes a kind of immortality ideology that assuages the nagging, not quite conscious terror of death.

4.6 The Case of Fundamentalism

This volume began with a survey of alternative and overlapping definitions of culture. The author finds two of these as related and compelling. Culture as a "roadmap for living" and "culture as a psychological defense against the terror inherent in our human condition." It is not proposed that the human condition is comprised solely of "terror" but it is certainly present in addition to the "wonder and awe" also embedded in the human condition and observable in the eyes of young children. The psychological defense referred to that is culture buffers the human from the "terror" produced by our cognitive awareness of our mortality and inevitable physical annihilation. Culture offers a possibility of constructing such a defense by providing a coherent description of reality that describe the nature of reality and identifies standards to achieve that if achieved and the cultural worldview believed provides the individual with sense of having value in a meaningful world. The cultural world view describes the "what" of reality. It also provides guidance for how to live a life of value and significance. It provides, if believed, a roadmap for living. The construction of the psychological defense has been called a "cultural anxiety buffer," (Salzman, 2001) within which are standards of value to achieve and guide us in our lives. Absent belief in a coherent worldview or the perception that one is living up to its standards of value we are subject to what may be called unmediated existential terror. It is proposed that this terror is the anxiety lurking in the background of our human condition. This anxiety is existential and associated with the possibility of the ultimate futility of our strivings in the face of our mortality. This terror/anxiety is obviously a highly aversive state that motivates behaviors that will reduce the intensity of this aversive state. Often the behaviors expressed can be extremely destructive and self-defeating. Alcohol and substance abuse are examples of terror management strategies may produce destructive consequences that may ultimately motivate more behaviors that only exacerbate the problem of unmediated existential terror. Perhaps the best solution to the "terror" inherent in the human condition is to embrace the "wonder" that is also part of the human condition.

It is proposed that culture provides pathways and roadmaps toward a buffer that is adaptive to the particular ecological niche it responds to. But what happens when the cultural worldview is shattered by trauma, discredited or not believed in or what happens if faith in the worldview is maintained but one does not perceive him or her as meeting its standards? An alternative worldview may be sought or constructed. The belief in the worldview may be bolstered through orthodoxy or fundamentalism.

Fundamentalism "is unusually capable of providing meaning through giving a sense of coherence to a fragmented world (Stevens, 2002, p. 34)" by providing a unifying philosophy of life and by meeting the human need for meaning. In human history great tides of change have produced great technological advances as well the angst that emerges from change and the tearing of the social and cultural fabric. Industrialization was one such tidal change where agrarian societies and the cultures that reflected and supported them gave way to wrenching migrations from the land and the shaking of the cultural foundations of life. Such anxiety producing change and the uncertainty of how to *be* and *act* in the new reality is an anxiety-fueled retreat to cultural and religious fundamentalism providing a sense of certainly and clarity while exacerbating the potential for inter-cultural or religious conflict that plagues the world today. Fundamentalism is not the province of a particular religion or cultural orientation it is proposed here as anxiety driven response to a perceived threat to the very foundations of a life of meaning and the possibility of constructing a sense of value or self-esteem thereby exposing people to unmediated existential anxiety.

A meaning system may endow one's life with personal significance and allows an individual to see oneself as having significance and value. For fundamentalists, then, religion or other immortality ideologies are a total and all encompassing way of life. They are closed systems. Fundamentalism provides certainty and clear and accessible standards to guide one through the confusion of modern life. The notion of multiple truths or relative truths may not be particularly comforting for people with certain dispositional characteristics under conditions of threat and fear. Altemeyer and Hunsberger (1992) define fundamentalism as the belief that: there is one set of religious teachings that clearly contains the fundamental, basic, intrinsic, essential, inerrant truth about humanity and deity; that this essential truth is fundamentally opposed by forces of evil which must be vigorously fought; that this truth must be followed today according to the fundamental, unchangeable practices of the past; and that those who believe and follow these fundamental teachings have a special relationship with the deity (pp. 118)." So fundamentalists of all types believe that they are opposed by forces of evil that must be confronted and defeated. In what contexts may fundamentalisms thrive?

Salzman (2008) and others have suggested that "globalization" is, perhaps, the meta-context of our time. Friedman (2000) metaphorically represented how contextual and ecological change may unsettle and disrupt people's sense of meaning and significance as the *Lexus and the Olive Tree* where the Lexus represents the forces of globalization and its accompanying ideology of *market fundamentalism* (Soros, 1998) and the *Olive Tree* represents traditional cultures and its prescribed pathways to meaning and a sense of value and significance. He suggests that the *Olive Tree* is being threatened and uprooted by the forces of globalization as represented by the *Lexus*. He describes the threat to traditional sources of meaning and value (the Olive Tree) eloquently:

> Olive trees are important. They represent everything that roots us, anchors us, identifies us and locates us in the world-whether it be belonging to a family, a community, a tribe, a nation, a religion or, most of all, a place called home. Olive trees are what give us the warmth of family, the joy of individuality, the intimacy of personal rituals, the depth of private relationships as well as the confidence and security to reach out and encounter others. We fight so intensely at times over our olive trees because, at their best, they provide the feelings of self-esteem and belonging that are as essential for human survival as food in the belly. (p. 31)

Perhaps we can think of fundamentalisms and the phenomena of "terrorism" as the *Revenge or Defense of the Olive Trees*. He describes globalization (The Lexus) as the inexorable integration of markets, nation-states and technologies to a degree never witnessed before in a way that is enabling individuals, corporations and nation-states to reach around the world farther, faster, deeper and cheaper than ever before. He observes that the process of globalization is also producing a powerful backlash from those brutalized or left behind by this new system. The driving idea behind globalization is free market capitalism. Globalization has its own dominant culture and ideology, which is why it tends to be homogenizing to a certain degree.

4.7 Globalization, Social Identity Theory and Self-Esteem Threat

According to Social Identity Theory (Tajfel & Turner, 1986) this homogenization may threaten sources of identity and self-esteem offered by social and cultural identifications and perceptions of distinctiveness. Social Identity Theory (SIT) holds that there is a strong tendency in people to divide the social world into "us" and "them." SIT proposes that individuals seek to enhance their self-esteem by identifying with specific social groups and that self-esteem is enhanced only to the extent that the persons involved perceive these groups as distinct and somehow superior to other competing groups. This perspective implies that the homogenizing effects of globalization may threaten the distinctiveness of important groups (i.e., clan, tribe, nation, religion) through which people seek to enhance the vital psychological resource and anxiety-buffer known as self-esteem. When the distinctiveness and presumptive superiority of one's group is threatened a strong defensive reaction is likely. Humans apparently need something larger than self to belong to and identify with. Group identification, then, is both the foundation of intergroup conflict and a primary source of self-esteem.

Crime, violence, fundamentalism and xenophobia often come to the fore in societies where the traditional patterns of family and community have been disrupted. A hegemonic global capitalism and its cultural impositions produce such disruption. These problems are exacerbated by the sense of inferiority that arises in people who perceive themselves as not living up to the standards that define value in the new system while the forces of globalization threaten their faith in traditional sources of meaning and value that cultural values and religious belief systems provide. As economic globalization has accelerated in the post-Cold War era, new categories of winners and losers have been produced along with a rise in fundamentalism, hyper-ethnocentrism and the proliferation of neo-fascist and right-wing extremist organizations (Lee, 2000). In the late nineteenth and early twentieth century such was the case when the technology-driven revolution unleashed by the industrial revolution physically and psychologically uprooted, dislocated and marginalized millions of people. Among its products were the rise of religious fundamentalism (i.e., Protestant fundamentalism in the U.S.), alternative worldviews, and political ideologies such as fascism and communism. These worldviews were attractive to millions because they addressed unmet human psychological needs as well as promising to alleviate material deprivation and offering psychological sustenance. These belief systems and ideologies offer psychological sustenance in the form of a meaning system and are therefore, a foundation for the construction of essential self-esteem and a sense of significance which was identified by Adler (see Ansbacher & Ansbacher, 1946) as the central organizing principle of our psychological strivings. Salzman (2008) concluded that fundamentalism is an anxiety driven response and may be seen as an alternative ideology, that is an anxiety driven response to constructed to find meaning and a sense of self-value in a worldview that offers people clear and accessible standards of value that if achieved provide an anxiety-buffer against the terror inherent in human existence. An extreme example of this motive is the religious martyr who is promised literal heroic death transcendence by adhering to the worldview and seeing one self as achieving its achieving its standards. This may be a compelling motive for those experiencing humiliation and live lives devoid of accessible sources of anxiety buffering self-esteem in a world of meaning.

In summary, humans share universal concerns and basic needs. Resident in the human condition is anxiety emanating from our awareness of our mortality in contradiction to the universal striving for continued existence. Human needs include the need for meaning in life. Culture(s) serve as a buffer to the anxiety inherent in the human condition a may serve as a psychological defense against this existential problem by offering a roadmap for living derived from the culture itself. This roadmap indicates how one should live and be in this life if one believes in the worldview and sees oneself as achieving its standards. Absent a meaningful worldview or the ability to achieve its standards (i.e., being poor in a materialist culture) exposing one to unmediated existential anxiety that may produce destructive behavioral compensations.

References

Altemeyer, B., & Hunsberger, B. (1992). Authoritarianism, religious fundamentalism, quest, and prejudice. *The International Journal for the Psychology of Religion, 2*(2), 113–133.

Ansbacher, H., & Ansbacher, R. (1946). *The individual psychology of Alfred Adler*. New York: Basic Books.

Baumeister, R. (1991). *Meanings of life*. New York: Guilford.

Becker, E. (1971). *The birth and death of meaning* (2nd ed.). New York: Free Press.

Becker, E. (1973). *The denial of death*. New York: Free Press.

Becker, E. (1975). *Escape from evil*. New York: Free Press.

Camus, A. (1955). *An absurd reasoning the myth of Sisyphus and other essays*. New York, NY: Vintage Books.

Friedman, T. (2000). *The lexus and the olive tree*. New York: Anchor Books.

Goldhagen, D. J. (1997). *Hitler's willing executioners: Ordinary Germans and the Holocaust*. New York: Vintage.

Greenberg, J., Solomon, S., & Pyszczynski, T. (1997). Terror management theory of self-esteem and cultural worldviews: Empirical assessments and conceptual refinements. In M. P. Zanna (Ed.), *Advances in experimental social psychology* (p. 139). San Diego, CA: Academic Press.

Heintzelman, S. J., & King, L. A. (2014). Life is pretty meaningful. *American Psychologist, 69*(6), 561–574. https://doi.org/10.1037/a0035049.

Kluckhohn, F. R. (1950). Dominant and substitute profiles of cultural orientations: Their significance for the analysis of social stratification. *Social Forces, 28*, 376–393.

Lee, M. A. (2000). *The beast reawakens: Fascism's resurgence from Hitler's spymasters to today's neo-Nazi groups and right-wing extremisms*. Abingdon, New York: Routledge.

Maslow, A. H. (1968). Music education and peak experience. *Music Educators Journal, 54*(6), 72–171.

McAdams, D. P. (2013). How actors, agents, and authors find meaning in life. In K. D. Markman, T. Proulx, & M. J. Lindberg (Eds.), *The psychology of meaning* (pp. 171–190). Washington, DC: American Psychological Association. https://doi.org/10.1037/14040-000.

Salzman, M. B. (2001). Globalization, culture & anxiety: Perspectives and predictions from terror management theory. *Journal of Social Distress and the Homeless, 10*(4), 337–352. https://doi.org/10.1023/A:1011676025600.

Salzman, M. B. (2008). Globalization, religious fundamentalism and the need for meaning. *International Journal of Intercultural Relations, 32*(4), 318–327.

Schimel, J., Hayes, J., Williams, T., & Jahrig, J. (2007). Is death really the worm at the core? Converging evidence that worldview threat increases death-thought accessibility. *Journal of Personality and Social Psychology, 92*(5), 789–803. https://doi.org/10.1037/0022-3514.92.5.789.

Shweder, R. A. (1991). *Thinking through cultures: Expeditions in cultural psychology*. Cambridge: Harvard University Press.

Solomon, S., Greenberg, J., & Pyszczynski, T. (1991). A terror management theory of social behavior: the psychological functions of self-esteem and cultural worldviews. In M. P. Zanna (Ed.), *Advances in experimental social psychology* (pp. 91–159). San Diego: Academic Press.

Soros, G. (1998). *The crisis of global capitalism*. New York: Public Affairs.

Stevens, M. J. (2002). The unanticipated consequences of globalization: Contextualizing terrorism. In C. E. Stout (Ed.), *The psychology of terrorism* (Vol. 3, pp. 31–56). London: Praeger.
Tajfel, H., & Turner, J. (1986). The social identity theory of intergroup behavior. In S. Worchel & L. W. Austin (Eds.), *Psychology of intergroup relations*. Chicago: Nelson-Hall.

Chapter 5
A Psycho-Existential View of Culture

Culture and the need for a "world of meaning to in which to act"
An essential psychological function of culture.
Terror Management Theory (TMT)
Empirical tests of TMT hypotheses, implications of findings.

5.1 Culture and the Need for a "World of Meaning to Act in"

A central proposition of this book is that culture(s) have important characteristics and functions that address core human concerns and needs. At the outset of this volume, multiple definitions of "culture" were considered and two became the focus of this narrative. It was asserted that humans have an existential need to know how to *be* and *act in the world* ...that humans need a *roadmap for living* and that culture(s) serve as a psychological defense against the terror inherent in the human condition. Culture(s) serve this essential function by providing a worldview that may be internalized that offers standards that if achieved allows for the construction of self-esteem. Self-esteem, the conviction that one has value in a meaningful world, serves as defense against the potentially crippling anxiety that is resident in the human condition due to our cognitive complexity that allows for the realization of our mortality. The conviction that one is of value in a meaningful world (self-esteem) is proposed as a human need that is addressed and constructed culturally. A previous chapter described how Buddhism, Confucianism and Judaism describe reality and offer a roadmap for being and acting in the world. This chapter will focus on how culture(s) serve as a psychological defense against existential terror. Selected evidence for this proposition extracted from the hundreds of empirical tests of hypotheses developed from Terror Management Theory (TMT) will be presented and the implications and applications of this compelling theory will be suggested and examined. Central to this examination is the foundational question of *What do humans really need* and how do culture(s) address them. Following this discussion, we will

M.B. Salzman, *A Psychology of Culture*, International and Cultural Psychology,
https://doi.org/10.1007/978-3-319-69420-7_5

examine the psychological and behavioral consequences that happens when a people's culture is traumatically disrupted and the world of meaning is shattered or the standards of value described by that description of reality become inaccessible.

We humans have a problem...an existential problem.

The human condition has been studied and pondered over time and geography. Humans are unique in their awareness of their ultimate and inevitable physical annihilation. We share, with all other biological beings, the basic motive to continue living but are unique in our awareness of mortality and the impossibility of achieving this basic biological motive to continue existence (Solomon, Greenberg, & Pyszcyznski, 1991). Mortality is undoubtedly a universal fact across cultures and geography but beliefs about this inevitable universal destiny vary. All seem to offer a potential buffer against the "terror" inherent in this aspect of the human condition.

The ideas of Ernest Becker (1971, 1973, 1975) and the overarching theory they produced (Terror Management Theory) consider the relationships among cultural factors, the terror inherent in human existence, and self-esteem. Anxiety is part of the human condition and responses to this aversive state vary from the courageous to the destructive. Recall that the cultural anxiety buffer requires that the individual or community have faith in the cultural or religious worldview and to see himself or herself as meeting its standards. So by maintaining faith in the cultural worldview and living up to its standards the individual is able to avoid the confrontation with the anxiety and "terror" inherent in the human condition that results from our awareness of our inability to live and continue existence. This "terror" may be managed by the construction, internalization and maintenance of cultural worldviews that prescribe standards of behavior and behavior for its adherents. If faith in the worldview is strong and beliefs about reality shared, humans may be provided with a sense that one is a person of value in a world of meaning. This conviction derived from cultural beliefs and achieving its standards of behavior is "self-esteem" which serves as a buffer from the potentially crippling anxiety that lurks below the surface of awareness. From this existential perspective (Becker 1971, 1973, 1975) the need for self-esteem is universal albeit constructed differently across cultures by adhering to the individuals' internalized conception of the standards of value that are prescribed by the culture. Terror management theory (TMT) proposes that a primary function of "self-esteem" is to buffer anxiety and specifically to buffer the anxiety resulting from our awareness of our inability to achieve the basic biological motive to continue life and existence. The inverse nature of the relationship between anxiety and self-esteem has been well documented (see Solomon et al., 1991 for review). Proponents of TMT maintain that cultural belief systems provide effective means of anxiety management by creating the illusion of "symbolic…or literal immortality" (Goldenberg, Pyszczynski, Greenberg, & Solomon, 2000, p. 201)." Literal immortality is often promised by religion. People who live according to the standards of the particular worldview and believe in that worldview faithfully are offered eternal life. Symbolic immortality may be achieved by perceiving oneself as a valued part of a culture that endures beyond one's mortal life or by producing great and enduring works of art, literature or soaring, transcendent architecture. Immortality may be sought through the children we produce or perhaps the books that we write. Becker (1975) thought that "culture itself is sacred, since it is the 'religion' that assures, in some way, the perpetuation of its members (p. 4)" either literally or symbolically. In this sense culture embodies the transcendence of death in some form or another. Becker (1971) and others have concluded that virtually all cultures are fundamentally spiritual or religious in character. He also suggested that one culture is a potential threat to another because it represents a competing immortality ideology. The ferocity of religious warfare and cultural conflicts may be explained by the high psychological stakes involved. People tend to take their immortality ideologies seriously.

The explanatory power of Becker's ideas and TMT is impressive. The lure of religious fundamentalism is a case in point because fundamentalism "is unusually capable of providing meaning through giving a sense of coherence to a fragmented world (Stevens, 2002, p. 34)" by providing a unifying philosophy of life and by meeting the human need for meaning and by providing believers with accessible standards of value providing a pathway to literal or symbolic immortality. A worldview infused with meaning and accessible standards of value provided by the worldview is a pre requisite for the construction of anxiety-buffering self-esteem. As noted, anxiety is a part of the human condition given our "existential problem." For the discouraged and disenfranchised it is essential the worldview prescribed standards of value be accessible. In the extreme we may see that racist ideologies and worldviews have very achievable standards. All one needs is, to be the "right" color, race, or ancestry.

"It is significant that, in Europe and the United States, right-wing extremists campaign, first and foremost, as protectors of Western Europe's cultural identity and economic prosperity (Salzman, 2001, p. 389)" thus gaining access to anxiety buffering self-esteem by bolstering a threatened cultural world view through the derogation of the different "other." This is echoed in the United States by calls to battle to fight the "culture wars." These arguments find receptive ears in the marginalized who cannot achieve anxiety-buffering self-esteem in the global capitalist system which is relatively miserly in its provision of this essential psychological resource. TMT predicts that such people, produced in growing numbers, will seek psychological sustenance in alternative world-views that they find compelling enough to have faith in and where they see themselves as meetings its standards of value thus assuaging the toxicity of unbuffered existential terror. The ideologies constructed by neo-Nazi, white supremacist, and religiously fundamentalist groups addresses such needs albeit in potentially dangerous and destructive ways.

5.2 Implications: Ecology, Culture, Self Esteem and Terror Management

Triandis (1994) placed culture in a context anchored in the ecology from which it arose and adapted. Globalization may be seen as the dominant ecological context of our time. The exigencies of global capitalism and its cultural impositions seem to allow for a small minority of the world's people to see themselves as of value in a meaningful universe according to the standards embedded in the cultural worldview. People seen as winners are celebrated in capitalist culture and losers are disparaged and even despised. The apparent failure of communism as an alternative system has not solved the problems of global capitalism and its attendant instability, inequities and psychological consequences. It is a system that continues to produce inequality, inequities and masses of marginalized people who cannot see themselves as having value in the system. In a materialistic culture, value is determined by one's relative wealth and possession. The poor, if they buy into this worldview, would find it difficult to achieve a sense of personal value in a meaningful world. They will therefore face the terror inherent in human existence unbuffered by self-esteem and be susceptible to intolerable anxiety and inferiority feelings that will be addressed for better or worse.

Solomon et al. (1991) suggested that there may be circumstances under which individuals cannot maintain the cultural anxiety-buffer, either because they cannot achieve a sense of value within the cultural drama, or because their faith in the cultural drama itself is shattered. In a global capitalist system and culture which guarantees that great numbers of the world's peoples will perceive themselves as "losers" in the great competition, a sense of value and self-esteem will be achieved only by the relatively few who perceive themselves as "winners" and who have faith in the world view described by global capitalism and its ideology of market fundamentalism. Indeed, globalization-proponent Friedman (2000) notes that analysts have "been wondering for a while now whether the turtles who are left behind by globalization, or most brutalized or offended by it, will develop an alternative ideology to liberal, free-market capitalism (p. 324)." He reminds us that there is historical precedent "in the first era of globalization when the world first experienced the creative destruction of global capitalism, the backlash eventually produced a whole new set of ideologies—communism, socialism, fascism—that promised to take the sting out of capitalism particularly for the average working person (p. 324)." That sting is psychological as well as material. People whose faith in a world-view is lost or shattered are placed in a state of psychological stress even if they perceive themselves as meeting its standards of value. Greider (1998) observed that the process of globalization is revolutionizing the world as its forces overwhelm domestic politics and national sovereignty. Its consequences dislocate and disrupt national cultures whose people often feel more loss than gain. It represents, perhaps, the meta-context of our time and it behooves social scientists to study the process and address its consequences.

Experimental social psychologists (see Greenberg, Solomon, & Pyszczynski, 1997; Solomon et al., 1991) have produced a substantial body of evidence from hundreds of empirical studies that suggest that cultures respond to core existential human concerns (i.e., mortality), that culture serves as an essential psychological defense against existential terror and that its traumatic disruption has predictable psychosocial consequences. The experimental design used in these studies is strongest in its internal validity as it allows for the inference of causality. Replication of the results of multiple studies with diverse populations may enhance the generalizability or external validity to populations beyond the laboratory. The similar consequences of cultural disruption and trauma in natural environments provide evidence of the external validity of the basic propositions.

5.3 Empirical Tests of TMT Hypotheses, Implications of Findings

TMT has generated testable hypotheses that have been supported empirically in many studies both national and internationally. The first central hypothesis derived from TMT (the anxiety-buffer hypothesis) is that if a psychological structure provides protection against anxiety, then augmenting that structure should reduce anxiety in response to subsequent threats. Numerous studies have tested this hypothesis (i.e., Greenberg et al., 1993). The second central hypothesis (the mortality salience hypothesis) derived from TMT is that, if faith in the cultural worldview and self-esteem function to protect people from anxiety about death, then reminders of this primary fear should increase people's need for these psychological structures.

Early tests of TMT hypotheses supported its predictions that self-esteem serves as an anxiety buffer against mortality salience (the anxiety buffer hypothesis). For example, when self-esteem of subjects was raised through false positive feedback on personality or intelligence tests and mortality was made salient by showing graphic footage of an autopsy subjects self-reported reduced anxiety in comparisons with control subjects and elevated self-esteem also reduced physiological arousal (as measured by skin conductance) in anticipation of the threat of electric shocks (Greenberg, Pyszczynski, Simon, & Chatel, 1992). Early tests of the mortality salience hypothesis showed that the manipulated condition of mortality salience produced the effect of increased affection and attraction to people who uphold our beliefs and an equally vigorous hostility and disdain for those who challenge or do not share our beliefs. Researchers have conceptualized these results as "worldview defense" to explain the exaggerated evaluations of similar and different others following the invocation of the mortality salience conditions.

Another early test of the mortality salience hypothesis (Greenberg et al., 1990) had Christian subjects evaluate Christian and Jewish targets after a mortality salience or control condition induction. These participants in the MS condition reported greater fondness for the Christian target and more adverse reactions to the Jewish target. Numerous studies have reported this effect. Later studies as well as current and historical events support the TMT proposition that under conditions of mortality salience anxiety prone humans tend to evaluate different others negatively in favor of one's own cultural worldview. This negative evaluation provokes the tendency to derogate, assimilate, or even annihilate those who do not support one's conception of reality

Recall that the mortality salience hypothesis states that if cultural worldviews and self-esteem provide beliefs about the nature of reality that function to assuage the anxiety associated with the awareness of death then asking people to ponder their own mortality (mortality salience) the need for the protection provided by these beliefs should increase. Empirical tests of these hypotheses have been supported.

These studies have supported the proposition that mortality salience increases positive reactions to those who uphold or validate the individual's worldview and negative reactions to those who violate or challenge the individual's worldview (i.e., Greenberg et al., 1990). There is also evidence that mortality salience may motivate aggression against those who do not support one's worldview that is a component of the cultural anxiety buffer. A vigorous reaction can be expected when a psychological defense is threatened.

When faith in belief systems is shaken or threatened or if the standards of value prescribed by the believed (faith intact) worldview are not achieved or achievable the resultant unbuffered anxiety creates an aversive affective condition that requires "terror management" responses. These defensive responses may be quite destructive (i.e., the tendency to derogate, demonize, or seek to harm the "other"). Pyszczynski et al. (2006) published an experimental study called "Mortality Salience, Martyrdom, and Military Might: The Great Satan versus the Axis of Evil." They investigated the effect of mortality salience on support for martyrdom attacks among Iranian college students and on the willingness of American students to support extreme military action with heavy "collateral damage." The MS condition increased the support for both as opposed to diplomatic action. It is interesting how each side attributes "evil" to the "other." Much blood has been shed in wars purporting to rid the world of "evil" and, we are reminded, that when war starts mortality is salient and the demonization of the "other" is provoked. This may explain why wars are so apparently easy to start and difficult to stop. So much for saber rattling.

Another example of a test of the anxiety-buffer and mortality salience hypotheses in Varanasi India where mortality salience is chronic and pervasive as some 250 public cremations take place along the Ganges daily (Fernandez, Castano, & Singh, 2010). They investigated in-group identification and cultural worldview defense between two groups of Hindus with naturally occurring high vs. low death exposure. In each group half were reminded about death and half of a control topic. They found increased cultural worldview defense and identification with India in the low exposure group but not in the high exposure group that showed consistently higher levels on these variables across conditions. These findings led the investigators to conclude that chronic death exposure may lead to chronic cultural worldview defense rather than acceptance of the inevitability of death.

As indicated earlier, more recent studies looking at the role of death thought accessibility (DTA) found that threats to the meaning and value-conferring constructs that are prescribed by the internalized cultural worldview increase the accessibility of death related thoughts (DTA) which motivate terror management defenses toward the threat. Terror management defenses, as noted, may include the distancing, derogation, demonization or even annihilation of the "other" who does not support or share our worldviews. We may consider this in relation to the ferocity of the "culture wars" in the United States that were manifest in the 2016 elections and intercultural conflict in general. Barak Obama, for example, was heavily criticized and even demonized in his first presidential campaign for making the observation that people, under conditions of stress and anxiety tend to cling to their cultural symbols which for many Americans are guns and religion or antipathy to people who aren't like them or anti-immigrant sentiment or anti-trade sentiment as a way to explain their frustrations. This observation is totally consistent with TMT perspectives. Below is an example of demonization of Obama displayed at an election rally.

So, TMT proposes that cultural worldviews and self-esteem derived from those worldviews protect people from their fear of death. Research has shown that threatening peoples' worldviews, or even reminding people that worldviews different from their own do exist, elicits both increased accessibility of death-related thoughts and hostility toward those who hold divergent worldviews. However, the content of a people's worldview matters and the centrality and saliency of values such as compassion and tolerance have consequence. Early TMT (Greenberg et al., 1992, 1992) research has shown that death reminders can increase tolerance and reduce hostility among people who hold the values of compassion and tolerance as central aspects of their worldviews. Research and educational policies may be informed by these findings and activate a sense of tolerance, compassion common humanity that can moderate defensive responses to cultural and worldview differences. There are other mitigating and moderating factors that may serve to reduce the potentially destructive effects of mortality salience and worldview defense. These, in addition to salience of the value of tolerance, include high dispositional or manipulated self-esteem (Harmon-Jones et al., 1997), a strong belief in symbolic immortality (Florian & Mikulincer, 1998), and a secure attachment orientation (Mikulincer & Florian, 2000). This line of research offers hope that educational interventions and the priming of our higher values may moderate our more destructive potentials.

If the studies testing hypotheses generated from TMT support the proposition that culture serves as a psychological defense against the "terror" inherent in the human condition what happens when faith in a worldview is weakened or shattered? What happens if the faith is maintained but one doesn't see him or herself as meeting its standards of value? What if the worldview is still believed but the person is blocked from meeting its standards by impediments such as racism or sexism? In both cases the buffer is weakened, shattered or rendered porous and anxiety and its consequence ensue. If culture serves as a psychological defense against the terror inherent in the human condition, then the effects of a traumatic disruption of a cultural anxiety buffer would open the individual or community to unmediated "existential terror" and anxiety. The implications of this proposition are profound. The traumatic disruption of indigenous people's cultures and its consequences shall be considered in the next chapter.

In addition to the internal validity strength of experimental designs we can observe the relevance of the theory in the non-laboratory natural settings such as the American reaction to the 9/11 attacks and attitudes toward the French rejection of the Iraq war and the "culture wars" in the United States. Huntington (1997) suggested that the forces of globalization and integration in the world are generating counterforces of cultural assertion and conflict among culturally distinct civilizations. He argued that post-Cold War global politics is being reconfigured along cultural differences and that the fault lines between civilizations, which are the broadest cultural entities, are becoming the central points of conflict in the world today. Such conflicts, he asserts, are uniquely dangerous and are shaped by cultural factors. They "tend to be violent and ugly, with both sides engaging in massacres, terrorism, rape and torture. The territory at stake is for one or both sides is a highly charged symbol of their history and identity, sacred land to which they have an inviolable right: The West Bank, Kashmir, Nagorno-Karabakh, the Drina Valley, Kosovo" (p. 252). He suggests that an upsurge in ethno-cultural conflict has occurred as the Cold War wound down. An understanding of the potency of the dynamics fueling intercultural conflict requires an examination of the essential psychological functions that cultures serve anxiety-prone human creatures. Cultural homogenization and integration as represented by "globalization" may represent a threat to vital sources of self-esteem provoking a fundamentalist reaction to the perceived threat to one's group identity.

Another theoretical perspective offers insight into these dynamics. Social Identity Theory (Tajfel & Turner, 1986) suggests that humans derived the vital psychological resource known as "self-esteem" through their identification with and belonging to groups. Although Social Identity Theory (SIT) does not seem to indicate why people seek and need self-esteem it acknowledges the centrality of the self-esteem motive. SIT (Tajfel & Turner, 1986) holds that there is a strong tendency in people to divide the social world into "us" and "them." SIT proposes that individuals seek to enhance their self-esteem by identifying with specific social groups and that self-esteem is enhanced only to the extent that the persons involved perceive these groups as distinct and somehow superior to other competing groups. Therefore, the homogenizing effects of globalization may threaten the distinctiveness of important groups (i.e., clan, tribe, nation, and religion) through which people seek to enhance the vital psychological resource known as self-esteem. When the distinctiveness and presumptive superiority of one's group is threatened a strong defensive reaction is likely. Humans apparently need something larger than self to belong to and identify with. Group identification and the social consensus that supports it, then, are both the foundation of intergroup conflict and a primary source of self-esteem. Although SIT recognizes the power of the self-esteem motive it does not seem to explain why we need this psychological resource whereas TMT demonstrates that self-esteem serves as a psychological defense against the terror inherent in the human condition. A clear implication is that, consistent with the mortality salience hypothesis, religious fundamentalism may represent the augmentation of cultural/religious worldviews under the condition of threat as represented by globalization and its homogenizing and dislocating effects.

These ideas and their empirical supports lend credibility to the proposition that culture serves as psychological defense against the anxiety ("terror") inherent in the human condition by providing a cultural worldview and standards of being and acting in the world. In other words, cultures provide a roadmap for living. By living up to these standards and having faith in the cultural worldview self-esteem maybe constructed which serves as an anxiety buffer needed to assuage the terror resulting from our uniquely human awareness of the inevitability of our physical annihilation. Threats to the cultural anxiety-buffer may provoke the tendency to derogate, assimilate, demonize or annihilate the different other whose existence or practice may threaten one's faith in the source of the anxiety buffer. Religious warfare, fundamentalism and "culture wars" may be explained by this perspective.

In summary, this chapter described a psycho-existential view of culture in relation to the universal human need for meaning and the role of culture(s) in addressing that need by constructing and defending worldviews that offer the possibility of achieving the perception that one is a person of value in a world of meaning to act in. The chapter proposes that culture serves an essential psychological function by providing a culturally derived worldview and standards of being and behaving that if achieved AND the cultural worldview is believed in would buffer the person against the existential anxiety (terror) inherent in the human condition. The awareness of death engenders potentially debilitating terror that is "managed" by the development and maintenance of cultural worldviews: humanly constructed beliefs about reality shared by individuals that minimize existential dread by conferring meaning and value (Heintzelman & King, 2014). All cultures provide a sense that life is meaningful by offering an account of the origin of the universe, prescriptions for appropriate behavior, and assurance of immortality for those who behave in accordance with cultural dictates. Literal immortality is afforded by souls, heavens, afterlives, and reincarnations associated with all major religions. Symbolic immortality is obtained by being part of a great nation, amassing great fortunes, achieving noteworthy accomplishments, and having children.

As indicated, this psycho-existential perspective on culture is supported by hundreds of empirical studies testing the central hypotheses of Terror Management Theory (TMT). Early studies tested two hypotheses. The first central hypothesis derived from TMT (the anxiety-buffer hypothesis) is that if a psychological structure provides protection against anxiety, then augmenting that structure should reduce anxiety in response to subsequent threats. The second central hypothesis (the mortality salience hypothesis) derived from TMT is that, if faith in the cultural worldview and self-esteem function to protect people from anxiety about death, then reminders of this primary fear should increase people's need for these psychological structures.

The bulk of these studies have demonstrated that mortality salience increases positive reactions to those who uphold or validate the individual's worldview and negative reactions to those who violate or challenge the individual's worldview. We recall the era of "freedom fries" and intense reactions to France's refusal to accept the Iraq war in the wake of the attacks on the U.S. on 9/11. Those attacks induced the conditions of mortality salience and essentially provided a natural experiment demonstrating support for the theory. Further studies and conceptual refinements have been developed are available but the basic propositions have been supported.

When faith in belief systems is shaken or threatened or if the standards of value prescribed by the believed (faith intact) worldview are not achieved or achievable the resultant unbuffered anxiety creates an aversive affective condition that requires "terror management" responses that may be quite destructive (i.e., the tendency to derogate, demonize, or seek to harm the "other"). These findings support the proposition that cultures(s) serve as a psychological defense against the terror resident in the human conditions and provide a "roadmap for living" for anxiety-prone human creatures to navigate through life in relative equanimity.

What happens when a cultural anxiety-buffer is weakened or shattered by traumatic events? What happens when a culture is traumatically disrupted by contact with foreign invaders, diseases and rapid, inexplicable depopulation? The next chapter will consider, in the light of the previous analysis, the phenomenon of cultural trauma and recovery.

References

Becker, E. (1971). *The birth and death of meaning* (2nd ed.). New York: Free Press.

Becker, E. (1973). *The denial of death*. New York: Free Press.

Becker, E. (1975). *Escape from evil*. New York: Free Press.

Fernandez, S., Castano, E., & Singh, I. (2010). Managing death in the burning grounds of Varanasi, India: A terror management investigation. *Journal of Cross-Cultural Psychology, 41*(2), 182–194.

Florian, V., & Mikulincer, M. (1998). Symbolic immortality and the management of the terror of death: The moderating role of attachment style. *Journal of Personality and Social Psychology, 74*(3), 725–734.

Friedman, T. (2000). *The lexus and the olive tree*. New York: Anchor Books.

Goldenberg, J., Pyszczynski, T., Greenberg, J., & Solomon, S. (2000). Fleeing the body: A terror management theory perspective on the problem of human corporeality. *Personality and Social Psychology Review, 4*(3), 200–218.

Greenberg, J., Pyszczynski, T., Simon, S., & Chatel, D. (1992). Terror management and tolerance: Does mortality salience always intensify negative reactions to others who threaten one's worldview. *Journal of Personality and Social Psychology, 63*(2), 212–220.

Greenberg, J., Pyszczynski, T., Solomon, S., Pine, E., Simon, L., & Jordan, K. (1993). Effects of self-esteem on vulnerability-denying defensive distortions: Further evidence of an anxiety buffering function of self-esteem. *Journal of Experimental Social Psychology, 29*, 229–251.

Greenberg, J., Pyszczynski, T., Solomon, S., Rosenblatt, A., Burling, J., Lyon, S., et al. (1992). Assessing terror management analysis of self-esteem: Converging evidence of an anxiety-buffering function. *Journal of Personality and Social Psychology, 63*, 913–922.

Greenberg, J., Pyszczynski, T., Solomon, S., Rosenblatt, A., Veeder, M., Kirkland, S., et al. (1990). Evidence for terror management theory II: The effects of mortality salience on reactions to those who threaten or bolster the cultural worldview. *Journal of Personality and Social Psychology, 58*, 308–318.

Greenberg, J., Solomon, S., & Pyszczynski, T. (1997). Terror management theory of self-esteem and cultural worldviews: Empirical assessments and conceptual refinements. In M. P. Zanna (Ed.), *Advances in experimental social psychology* (Vol. 29). San Diego, CA: Academic Press.

Greider, W. (1998). *One world, ready or not: The manic logic of global capitalism*. New York: Simon and Schuster.

Harmon-Jones, E., Simon, L., Greenberg, J., Pyszczynski, T., Solomon, S., & McGregor, H. (1997). Terror management theory and self-esteem: Evidence that increased self-esteem reduces mortality salience effects. *Journal of Personality and Social Psychology, 72*, 24–36.

Heintzelman, S. J., & King, L. A. (2014). Life is pretty meaningful. *American Psychologist, 69*(6), 561–574. https://doi.org/10.1037/a0035049.

Huntington, S. P. (1997). *The clash of civilizations and the remaking of world order*. New York: Touchstone.

Mikulincer, M., & Florian, V. (2000). Exploring individual differences in reactions to mortality salience: Does attachment style regulate terror management mechanisms? *Journal of Personality and Social Psychology, 79*(2), 260.

Pyszczynski, T., Abdooahi, A., Greenberg, J., Solomon, S., Pyszczynski, T., Greenberg, J., et al. (2006). Mortality salience, martyrdom and military might: The great satan and the axis of evil. *Personality and Social Psychology Bulletin, 32*(4), 525–537.

Salzman, M. (2001). Globalization, culture & anxiety. *Journal of Social Distress and the Homeless, 10*(4), 337–352.

Solomon, S., Greenberg, J., & Pyszcyznski, T. (1991). A terror management theory of social behavior: The psychological functions of self-esteem and cultural worldviews. In M. P. Zanna (Ed.), *Advances in experimental social psychology* (pp. 91–159). San Diego: Academic Press.

Stevens, M. J. (2002). The unanticipated consequences of globalization: Contextualizing terrorism. In C. E. Stout (Ed.), *The psychology of terrorism* (Vol. 3, pp. 31–56). London: Praeger.

Tajfel, H., & Turner, J. C. (1986). The social identity theory of inter-group behavior. In S. Worchel & L. W. Austin (Eds.), *Psychology of intergroup relations*. Chicago: Nelson-Hall.

Triandis, H. C. (1994). *Culture and social behavior*.

Chapter 6
Cultural Trauma and Recovery

Cultural trauma and indigenous peoples
The motive for cultural recovery and reconstruction
The recovery of language, ceremonies, spirituality
Examples of the motive to recover and reconstruct culture following the traumatic disruption of culture

I became interested in Terror Management Theory (TMT) as a result of lived experience and work with Native people in Arizona (Navajo), Alaska (Alaskan Natives), and Hawai'i (Native Hawaiians). I became aware of the central importance of culture, cultural disruption and its consequences and the motivation to preserve and/or recover their cultures. In my work as a student, researcher, teacher, counselor and psychologist I tried to understand the meaning of my observations. I noted that (Salzman, 2001) peoples as genetically distinct as Yup'ik Eskimos, Navajo and Athabaskan Indians, Hawaiian Natives and Australian Aboriginals experienced similar physical, social, behavioral and psychological symptomologies (e.g., high rates of suicide, alcohol abuse and accidental death across vast distances and varied genetic inheritance (Austin & Marsella, 2005, Brave Heart & DeBruyn, 1998; Bushnell, 1993; Butlin, 1983; Farnsworth, 1997; Harris, 1990; Indian Health Service, 1995; Napoleon, 1996; Stannard, 1989). I found the theoretical lens of TMT and the empirical work supporting it provided a plausible explanation for my observations. A good theory should generate testable hypotheses and possess great explanatory power. I found TMT to possess both characteristics that illuminate the meaning of naturalistic and experimental data. It is an explanation derived from a view of the psychological functions of culture and its implications for behavior, mental health and well-being. All of the populations mentioned experienced dramatic and what must have been an inexplicable, traumatic depopulation. A "dying" that decimated the populations that traditional cultural mechanisms could not halt resulting from "contact" with European settlers and colonizers. All of the populations had their cultures assaulted, languages suppressed and traditional spirituality discredited. All of these populations, after enduring this microbial and cultural assault have engaged in movements of cultural recovery. How can we explain this?

M.B. Salzman, *A Psychology of Culture*, International and Cultural Psychology,
https://doi.org/10.1007/978-3-319-69420-7_6

Some key points have emerged from previous inquiries (Salzman, 2001, 2005; Salzman & Halloran, 2004):

- Indigenous cultures have been traumatically disrupted as a result of contact with Europeans.
- Culture infuses the world with meaning that allows for the construction of the conviction that one has value in a meaningful world ("self-esteem").
- Self- esteem is inversely related to anxiety and serves as a buffer against the against the terror inherent in the human condition (the knowledge that we are mortal and face inevitable physical annihilation).
- Cultures provide pathways to the construction of self-esteem for those who buy into the cultural worldview.
- Cultures serve as a psychological defense against existential terror. People are motivated to bolster their cultural worldview (CWV) and derogate those that do not support their CWV under existential threat. However, there may be circumstances under which individuals cannot maintain the cultural anxiety buffer, either because they cannot achieve a sense of value within the cultural drama or because their faith in the CWV is itself shattered.
- Cultures are a source of meaning and anxiety buffering self-esteem.
- When the cultural anxiety buffer is shattered (see description of the "Great Death" below) maladaptive attempts to manage the resultant anxiety may produce further tragedy and grief.
- Grief may be unresolved when traditional cultural solutions are suppressed or lost, contributing to the multigenerational transmission of trauma.
- Cultural recovery movements have been occurring among indigenous peoples throughout the world to reconstruct a world of meaning to act in, to make anxiety-buffering self-esteem accessible and to recover ceremonies, narratives and rituals that address life's problems.

This psycho-existential framework considers the relationships among cultural factors, the terror inherent in the human condition, and self-esteem. If culture serves as a psychological defense against the terror inherent in the human condition, then the effects of a traumatic disruption of a cultural anxiety buffer would open the individual or community with unmediated "existential terror and anxiety."

It is not surprising, then, to see that anxiety and anxiety "disorders" are so prevalent in Native America. Duran (2006) found that 58% of Native American clients at a Native American Health Center had anxiety disorders and he suggested that anxiety underlies all other problems that Indians are experiencing regardless of whether there was a concurrent substance abuse disorder. Manson et al. (1996) also note high rates of anxiety in American Indian populations across tribe and region. They also suggest, consistent with Brave Heart and DeBruyn (1998), the efficacy of traditional ceremonial treatment in addressing the traumatic experiences of Native American people noting that the "great relevance for such forms of healing lies in their meaning-making aspects and the coherence-engendering qualities of the healing ritual" (p. 275). They observe that such rituals are designed to promote a sense of continuity of the community and continuity of the individual in the culture.

Anxiety is part of the human condition and responses to this aversive state vary from the courageous to the destructive. Recall that the cultural anxiety buffer requires that the individual or community have faith in the cultural or religious worldview and to see himself or herself as meeting its standards. So by maintaining faith in the cultural worldview and living up to its standards the individual is able to avoid the confrontation with the anxiety and "terror" inherent in the human condition that results from our awareness of our inability to live and continue existence. The self-esteem anxiety-buffer is achieved and constructed by having faith and belief in the cultural worldview and seeing oneself as having achieved its standards of value. As noted, the cultures offer a roadmap to self-esteem by making "right action" and "right ways of being" (Becker, 1971) available to believers in the particular cultural (including religious) worldview. The need for a world of meaning to act in may also be addressed by weaving together aspects of multiple cultures into a coherent worldview which is believable by the individual and that offers accessible standards of value that are achievable.

6.1 Cultural Trauma

What happens when faith in a worldview is weakened or shattered? When a people's culture is traumatically disrupted its self-esteem constructing and prescribing functions are impaired and the person or community may be flooded with unmediated existential terror. This cultural trauma may be exacerbated by the imposition of colonial systems that are based on the presumed "inferiority" of the colonized and traumatized. The characteristics of a colonial situation bear mention as noted by Fanon (1968) who observed that: "When the Native is confronted with the colonial order of things he finds he is in a state of permanent tension. The settler's world is a hostile world which spurns the Native. The denigration of indigenous cultures and people, supported by military and institutional power and internalized by the colonized, has devastating consequences (p. 52). The colonial situation that often accompanies cultural trauma is relevant as the situational context is a powerful influence on the behavior, self-perceptions, worldviews and cognitions of both the colonized and the colonizer.

6.2 The Power of the Situation: The Colonial Context

Memmi (1965), in his classic work *The Colonized and the Colonizer* describes the psychological effects of colonialism on both the colonizer and the colonized in the case of the French colonization of Algeria. He saw that colonialism was harmful to both cultures. Memmi suggested that the colonial situation casts its actors in the roles of the colonizer and the colonized and it is this situation that is definitive. For these roles to change the situation must change. Memmi described the colonial situation as one that is based on economic privilege, despite suggestion of more noble goals of religious conversion or civilization. Its key tools are racism and terror. Racism is ingrained in every colonial institution, and establishes the "sub-humanity" of the colonized, fostering poor self-concepts in the colonized as well. He goes on to describe the dilemma of the colonizer who sees the injustice of the situation ("the colonizer who refuses") and the colonizer who, while being aware of his illegitimate privilege accepts his role as usurper relying on the conviction and presumption of his "superiority." The colonizer who refuses and recognizes the colonial system as unjust may withdraw from the conditions of privilege or remain to fight for change. Yet although he is benevolent, he is detached from the struggle of the colonized. This is a difficult position. The role of colonizer changes only when the situation changes.

Oppression may be internalized resulting in debilitating inferiority feelings. Inferiority feelings are inversely related to self-esteem and are highly aversive. People suffering inferiority feelings are motivated to escape them. There are multiple destructive compensations for chronic feelings of inferiority such as substance abuse and its correlates like domestic violence whose effects may be transmitted across generations. What happens if the faith is maintained but one doesn't see him or herself as meeting its standards of value? What if the worldview is still believed but the person is from blocked from meeting its standards by impediments such as racism or sexism? In both cases the buffer is weakened, shattered or rendered porous and anxiety and its consequences ensue.

6.3 Cultural Trauma in Alaska

Napoleon (1996) eloquently describes the destruction of cultural worldview of the Yup'ik people of western Alaska from the radical depopulation of the people from imported diseases such as what he called the "Great Death" in the early part of the twentieth century:

> The suffering, the despair, the heartbreak, the desperation, and confusion these survivors lived through is unimaginable. People watched helplessly as their mothers, fathers, brothers, and sisters grew ill, the efforts of the *angalkuq* failing. First one family fell ill, then another. The people grew desperate, the angalkuq along with them. Then the death started, with people wailing morning, noon, and night. Soon whole families were dead, some leaving only a boy or a girl. Babies tried to suckle on the breasts of dead mothers, soon to die themselves. Even the medicine men grew ill and died in despair with their people, and with them died a great part of *Yuuyaruq*, the ancient spirit world of the Eskimo. Whether the survivors knew or understood, they had witnessed the fatal wounding of *Yuuraruq* and the old Yup'ik culture...The Yup'ik world was turned upside down, literally overnight. Out of the suffering, in confusion, desperation, heartbreak, and trauma was born a new generation of Yup'ik people. They were born into shock. They woke to a world in shambles, many of their people and their beliefs strewn around them, dead. In their minds they had been overcome by evil. their medicines and their medicine men and women had proven useless. Everything they had believed in had failed. Their ancient world had collapsed...The world

> the survivors woke to was without anchor. They woke up in shock, listless, confused, bewildered, heartbroken, and afraid. (pp. 10–11).

Solomon, Greenberg, and Pyszczynski (1991) suggested that there may be circumstances under which individuals cannot maintain the cultural anxiety-buffer either because they cannot maintain a sense of value within the cultural drama, or because they can no longer sustain faith in the cultural drama itself. One possibility for such people is to find an alternative cultural worldview that is more compelling that better enables them to obtain self-esteem. The accession to the conversion pressures of the apparently dominant European worldview may be seen in this light (Salzman, 2001). Napoleon description is illustrative:

> When the first white men arrived in the Yup'ik villages, the people did not immediately abandon their old ways...but resistance to Western rule would crumble, Yuuyaraq would be abandoned, and the spirit world would be displaced by Christianity...The change was brought about as a result of the introduction of diseases that had been born in the slums of Europe...To these diseases the Yup'ik and other Native tribes had no immunity, and to these they would lose up to 60% of their people. As a result of the epidemics, the Yup'ik world would go upside down; it would end. (pp 10–11)

This is cultural trauma. It is the shattering of a world of meaning that offered clear behavioral and ontological prescriptions of how to be human. Napoleon (1996) is eloquent in describing the pre-contact culture of the Yup'ik people that was called "Yuuyaraq" which was translated as the "Way of the Human Being." Yuuyaraq was a world of meaning and a "roadmap for living" that was traumatically disrupted by imported disease that Napoleon called the "Great Death." He described it as follows:

> Prior to the arrival of Western people, the Yup'ik were alone in their riverine and Bering Sea homeland—they and the spirit beings that made things the way they were. They were ruled by the customs, traditions and spiritual beliefs of their people, and shaped by these and their environment: the tundra, the river and the Bering Sea...They called it *Yuuyaraq*, the way of being a human being. Although unwritten, this way can be compared to Mosaic law because it governed all aspects of the human being's life...It defined acceptable behavior for all members of the community (p. 4).

This description of a world infused with meaning with clear prescriptions of how to *be* a human being is consistent with the idea that culture provides a "roadmap for living" for anxiety prone human creatures that need to know how to live. The experience of the Yup'ik as described above was common throughout the indigenous world as Western colonizers made contact and spread deadly diseases that decimated the populations.

6.4 Cultural Trauma in Hawai‘i and the Pacific

In Hawai‘i the pre-contact population estimates ranged from 2000 to 1,000,000 people (Bushnell, 1993; Stannard, 1989). As in Alaska and throughout the indigenous world the effects of contact were disastrous for the population. The deadly diseases decimated the population and overwhelmed the indigenous system of healing as wave upon wave of epidemics struck the Hawaiian people beginning in 1804. The missionaries, as they did with Alaska Natives assisted the Hawaiians in attributing the cause of this disaster to the presumed sinful indigenous religious beliefs and practices. Ultimately traditional Hawaiian beliefs succumbed to the religion of the missionaries as the population declined dramatically to the point that the ultimate extinction of the people came to be regarded as inevitable (Davis, 1968). The experiences described above were common throughout the indigenous world. In the Pacific, waves of epidemics decimated and demoralized the indigenous populations. For example, on Pohnpei epidemics killed 50% of the population and in the New Hebrides the indigenous population was almost wiped out (Val, 1994). It was estimated that in 1788 there were about 1500 aborigines living around Sydney but Darwin in 1836 found only a few hundred remaining reflecting his observation that "Wherever the European has trod, death seems to pursue the aboriginal. We may look to the wide extent of the Americas, Polynesia, the Cape of Good Hope and Australia, and we find the same result (Moorehead, 1966, p. 169). So it seems that the "Great Death" in Native Alaska and the cultural collapse so vividly described by Napoleon was part of a much wider phenomena that may have produced similar consequences throughout the indigenous world.

Salzman and Halloran (2004) describe the experiences and consequences of cultural disruption of three genetically distinct and geographically dispersed indigenous groups. This contact and its attendant assaults by disease, economic, and cultural disruption have produced similar behavioral, health and well-being consequences (e.g., high rates of suicide, alcoholism, and accidental deaths) across vast distances and genetic inheritance. This is consistent with TMT's anxiety buffer hypothesis, which states that: if a psychological structure provides protection against anxiety, then augmenting that structure should reduce anxiety in response to subsequent threats. It follows then that a weakening of that structure (e.g., culture and cultural worldviews and it standards of value) would expose the individual to heightened anxiety that motivates often maladaptive anxiety management strategies such as substance abuse.

Also consistent with TMT's *anxiety buffer hypothesis* was that the traditional the old culture of the Hawaiians and its standards for living and being was not simply abandoned or surrendered. The traditional Hawaiian healers, the embodiment of the cultural worldview (CWV), fought back and defended the culture and its spirituality with increased vigor. There was an increase in the training and production of traditional healers as efforts were made to bolster the traditional system as predicted by TMT. However, they too died as noted by Bushnell (1993) "whatever course the Kahunas chose to follow proved inadequate to meet the needs of their stricken people. These events shattered faith in a culture that sustained them for centuries and in TMT terms making anxiety-buffering self-esteem inaccessible. The people, then, as anxiety prone human beings coped with this aversive condition by whatever means were accessible. There was mass conversion to Christianity and an increase in destructive anxiety related behaviors (i.e., alcohol abuse, domestic violence).

The traumatic disruption of the collective psychological defense that is culture produces predictable consequences including an increase of anxiety and the motivation to engage in anxiety-reducing behaviors that are often destructive and maladaptive. Such behaviors may have the temporary palliative effect of reducing anxiety but tend to produce additional sources of grief, pain and tragedy (Department of Education, 1993). Absent traditional mechanisms for dealing with grief and tragedy (e.g., grieving ceremonies) the grief may be unresolved and transmitted across generations. Unresolved grief, without access to deeply resonant ceremony and ritual designed to address the existential problem that is grief, tends to produce maladaptive attempts to manage the pain (e.g., alcohol abuse, domestic violence) that only produces more tragedy and unresolved grief facilitating the multigenerational transmission of trauma (Brave Heart & DeBruyn, 1998).

6.5 Cultural Trauma in Aboriginal Australia

Prior to white colonial settlement in 1788, there were some 500 indigenous tribal groups in Australia, each with distinct languages and cultural practices. Common to all indigenous groups was the centrality of the land, family and kinship relationships and spirituality to their cultural worldviews (Christie, 1988). As a result of contact, depopulation due to imported diseases, colonization and policy these elements of the cultural worldviews were severely undermined.

The history of white settlement in Australia is plagued with its intervention into Aboriginal life and culture (see Ober, Peeters, Archer, & Kelly, 2000.). In the first century of settlement, these included land dispossession by force, theft of women, slavery and war, introduced diseases, and the missionary zeal for conversion of Aboriginal people and rejection of Aboriginal spiritual concepts such as the dreaming, a sacred, heroic time, long ago, when humans and nature came to be (Stanner, 1979). Moreover, settlement brought with it the assertion of the British legal system, which effectively extinguished indigenous customary law. In the twentieth century, further intervention into Aboriginal culture and life was evidenced in the Government's White Australia Policy and a general strategy of indigenous assimilation through forced removal of children from their family of origin and placement with Europeans, which undermined Aboriginal social structures (Koolmartie & Williams, 2000). Altogether, such interventions into Aboriginal life have been argued to represent a not too subtle form of cultural genocide (Human Rights and Equal Opportunity Commission, 1997). At the very least, the destruction of Aboriginal law, spirituality, social structure, and the possession of their land are widely regarded to have severely subverted their traditional cultural worldview (e.g., Ober et al., 2000; Wessels & Bretherton, 2000). The results were predictable and common throughout the Aboriginal communities. For example, in Australia's Northern Territories, domestic and family violence is the leading cause of admission to hospitals and that intentional self-harm is a major social problem in many indigenous communities in the indigenous communities in the Northern Territories of Australia (Markey, 1998; Reser, 2000). The colonial context imposed on these populations by invaders and settlers is defined by inferiority and superiority. Fanon

(1968) notes that "The settler keeps alive in the Native an anger which he deprives an outlet; the native is trapped in the tight links of the chains of colonialism" (p. 54). He observed, from his clinical work in colonial North Africa, that "The colonized man will first manifest this aggressiveness which has been deposited in his bones against his own people (p. 52)." Often, this tension is manifested in the family. Such are the predictable consequences of traumatic cultural disruption and the shattering of the cultural anxiety-buffer and consequent exposure to the existential terror resident in the human condition. The motive of indigenous peoples around the world to recover and reconstruct their cultures may be seen in this light. Movements of cultural recovery and renaissance may be seen as an effort to reconstruct a world of meaning to act in as indigenous peoples with similar histories of traumatic cultural disruption have sought and seek to identify bedrock principles and values that define their being and guide their action.

6.6 Cultural Recovery in Native Alaska

Inupiat Ilitqusiat is a social movement that became institutionalized in northwest Alaska during the 1980s. This term roughly translates as the "wisdom and lessons of Inupiaq people" (McNabb 1991, p. 63). This reformative and redemptive movement seeks positive social and individual change through the elimination of some facets of Western culture and relearning Native culture. The movement was anticipated by Inupiaq leader Willie Hensley's keynote speech at the 1980 Alaska Federation of Natives Convention who stated that:

> "We cannot look to corporate or political life to fill the void of a century of psychological repression...A renaissance of our language and culture will give us the basis for the renewal of our people. (p. 65)."

Elders Councils were established to recover and identify bedrock principles, rooted in traditional culture that would provide the basis for the esteem and confidence that are highly correlated with successful performance and adaptive action in the current realities. The movement identified values that define the "Inupiaq Way." These include such core values as sharing, respect for elders, cooperation, respect for others, knowledge of language, love of children, hard work, avoidance of conflict, respect for nature, spirituality, humor, hunter success, and humility. These core values were printed on wallet sized cards and distributed to Inupiaq people to serve as a reference of how to *be* consistent with the cultural standards defined by the "Inupiaq Way." We can see from this movement an effort to restore a "roadmap for living" and to clarify standards of value embedded in the Inupiaq cultural worldview. We can also interpret this, and other recovery movements, as an attempt to bolster the cultural anxiety buffer by offering those who believe in the "Inupiaq Way" a clear description of how to *be* and *act* in a world of meaning.

The recovery of traditional ceremonies addressing such existential life problems as grief is also a focus of the recovery. In the village of Minto in the interior of

Alaska an effort to resurrect a traditional grief ceremony, a memorial potlatch occurred under the direction of grieving parents who were elders of the community. They, in their grief of losing their son to an alcohol related "accident," wanted to demonstrate the ceremony so that the community might learn or remember this meaning making grieving ceremony. The multi-day ceremony was filmed for distribution titled "Hitting Sticks Healing Hearts" (Minto Village Council, 1991). This is an example of "cultural recovery."

6.7 The Hawaiian Renaissance

Kanahele (1982) saw the process of recovering and the reconstruction of Hawaiian culture as a psychological renewal and purging of feelings of alienation and inferiority as well as a reassertion of dignity. A cultural revival that began in Hawai'i in the late 1960s took off tremendously in the 1970s and continues to influence generations of Hawaiians today (Kanahele, 1982). During the Hawaiian Renaissance period, Hawaiians' interest in almost all aspects of Hawaiian culture, including music, hula, art, language, crafts, literature, religion and politics increased immensely. Kanahele (1982) writes:

> Like a dormant volcano coming to life again, the Hawaiians are erupting with all the pent-up energy and frustrations of a people on the 'make.' This great happening has been called a 'psychological renewal,' a 'reaffirmation,' a 'revival,' and a 'renaissance.' No matter what you call it, it is the most significant chapter in 20th century Hawaiian history. Why? Because it has reversed years of cultural decline; it has created a new kind of Hawaiian consciousness; it has inspired greater pride in being Hawaiian; it has led to bold and imaginative ways of reasserting our identity; it has led to a new political awareness; and it has had and will continue to have a positive impact on the economic and social uplifting of the Hawaiian community. (p. 10).

In the 1970s the construction, launching and successful navigation by traditional means of the voyaging canoe, the Hokule'a, is seen as a key milestone in the Hawaiian renaissance that was characterized by language and cultural recovery and a movement for political sovereignty. In the 1970s the Hokule'a sailed under the guidance of the stars, currents and winds to reach Tahiti. In the summer of 2017, the Hokule'a successfully returned from a 3 year round the world voyage using ancient Polynesian science and navigational techniques. The mission, touched 150 ports and 19 countries, was rooted in Hawaiian values that promoted a profound sense of caring for the health of the earth (Malama Honua). The first trip of the Hokule'a "helped catalyze a reawakening not only of Hawaiian culture but also of traditional Polynesian life throughout the Pacific" (Zunin, 2014, p. B6). The return of the Hokule'a in June of 2017 after circumnavigating the earth using ancient Hawaiian navigation techniques, while affirming the Hawaiian value of Malama Honua (caring for the earth), was celebratory and inspiring. It provided evidence of the brilliance and skill of the ancient navigators. The arrival capped a 3 year, 4600 mile world-wide voyage that operationalized Hawaiian values and spread the supreme value of *Aloha* around the world while supporting the health of the planet. It was a powerful and deeply resonant expression of cultural pride. Tens of thousands of people greeted the Hokule'a upon its emotional return to Hawai'i with ceremony, Hula, chanting, music and prayer. In the course of the journey new leadership was cultivated and more than two dozen apprentice navigators were trained thus ancient knowledge was transmitted across generations. Lessons learned from the voyage were brought into the classrooms and curriculum. This is a good example of cultural recovery along with the recovery of language, stories, spirituality and *Mana* (Honore, 2017).

The trauma from which these cultural recovery movements arise are common. In Polynesia and specifically the Marquesas, for example, traditional life is coming back from the brink of extinction. The Marquesans also had a world of meaning infused by their culture disrupted by the effects of epidemics of diseases that decimated the population. According to Zunin (2014) the Marqueas suffered the greatest population decline from diseases brought by Western contact. Zunin, a medical doctor and columnist for the Honolulu Star Advertiser writes that by the early twentieth century the eighteenth century Marquesan population of 78,000 was reduced to just 4000. Dr. Zunin is serving as medical officer on the two voyaging canoes on the first leg of their round the world journey to Tahiti as the request of the Polynesian Voyaging Society. This voyage as well as the recovery and use of language, identification of bedrock values and ways of living may be seen as efforts to reconstruct a "roadmap for living" and a cultural anxiety buffer that allows for the construction of a sense of value in a meaningful world whose meaning is infused by culture. This "roadmap for living" is communicated across cultures through practice, stories and historical narratives. When working in a Native Alaskan mental health and human services program the author came upon a book by an Athabaskan author titled "Distant Time Stories: Stories we live by." This seemed compelling because of the author's observation that an important component of cultural recovery seemed to be the recovery and telling of historic and cultural narratives or stories. The example of the Passover story was offered in a previous chapter. The next chapter will examine the structure and function of historical and cultural narratives that may facilitate the transmission of culture and historical memory across generations.

References

Austin, A., & Marsella, A. J. (2005). Understanding substance use and violent behavior in a Native Hawaiian community. In A. J. Marsella, A. Austin, & B. Grant (Eds.), *Social change and psychosocial adaptation in the Pacific Islands: Cultures in transition*. New York, NY: Springer.

Becker, E. (1971). *The birth and death of meaning: An interdisciplinary perspective on the problem of man* (2nd ed.). New York: Free Press.

Brave Heart, M. Y. H., & DeBruyn, L. M. (1998). The American Indian holocaust: Healing historical unresolved grief. *American Indian and Alaska Native Mental Health Research: The Journal of the National Center, 8*(2), 56–78.

Bushnell, A. O. (1993). *The gifts of civilization: Germs and genocide in Hawai'i*. Honolulu: University of Hawai'i Press.

Butlin, A. (1983). *Our original aggression*. Sydney, Australia: Allen & Unwin.

Christie, M. (1988). The invasion of Aboriginal education. In B. Harvey & S. McGinty (Eds.), *Learning my way: Papers from the national conference on adult Aboriginal learning*. Perth, Australia: Australian Government Publishing.

Davis, G. (1968). *A shoal of time: History of the Hawaiian islands*. Honolulu: University of Hawai'i Press.

Department of Education. (1993). *Hawai'i youth risk behavior survey report*. Honolulu, HI: Department of Educational, Office of Instructional Services/General Education Branch.

Duran, E. (2006). *Healing the soul wound: Counseling with American Indians and other native people*. New York: Teachers College Press.

Fanon, F. (1968). *The wretched of the earth*. New York, NY: Grove Press.

Farnsworth, C.M. (1997, June 8). Australians resist facing up to legacy of parting aborigines from families. *New York Times*, p. 10.

Harris, J. (1990). *One blood: 200 years of aboriginal encounter with Christianity; a story of hope*. Sutherland, Australia: Albatross Books.

Honore, M. (2017, June 18). Securing a legacy. *Honolulu Star Advertiser Commemorative Edition*, p. 2, 3.

Human Rights and Equal Opportunity Commission. (1997). *Bringing them home report of the national inquiry into the separation of Aboriginal and Torres Strait Islander children from their families*. Canberra: Australian Government Publishing Service.

Indian Health Service. (1995). *Trends in Indian health*. Washington, DC: U.S. Department of health and Human Services.

Kanahele, G. S. (1982). *Hawaiian renaissance*. Honolulu, HI: Project WAIAHA.

Koolmartie, J., & Williams, R. (2000). Unresolved grief and the removal of Indigenous Australian children. *Australian Psychologist, 35*, 158–166.

Manson, S., Beals, J., O'Neill, T., Piasek, J., Bechtold, D., Keane, E., et al. (1996). Wounded spirits, ailing hearts: PTSD and related disorders among American Indians. In A. J. Marsella (Ed.), *Ethnocultural aspects of posttraumatic stress disorder: Issues, research, and clinical application* (pp. 251–282). Washington, DC: American Psychological Association.

Markey, G. (1998). *The health status of women in the Northern Territory*. Darwin: Territory Health Services Women's Health Strategy Unit.

McNabb, S. (1991). Elders, Inupiat Ilitqusiat, and culture goals in northwest Alaska. *Arctic Anthropology, 8*(2), 63–76.

Memmi, A. (1965). *The colonizer and the colonized*. Boston, MA: Beacon Press.

Minto Village Council. (1991). *Hitting sticks healing hearts*. Manley Hot Springs, Alaska: River Tracks Productions.

Moorehead, A. (1966). *The fatal impact: An account of the invasion of the South Pacific* (pp. 1767–1840). New York, NY: Harper & Row.

Napoleon, H. (1996). *Yuuyaraq: The way of the human being*. Native Knowledge Network: Fairbanks, Alaska.

Ober, C., Peeters, L., Archer, R., & Kelly, K. (2000). Debriefing in different cultural frameworks: Responding to acute trauma in Australian Aboriginal contexts. In B. Raphael & J. P. Wilson (Eds.), *Psychological debriefing: Theory, practice and evidence*. Cambridge: Cambridge University Press.

Reser, J. P. (2000). Indigenous suicide in cross-cultural context: An overview statement and selective bibliography of sours relevant to Indigenous suicide in Australia, North America and the Pacific. *South Pacific Journal of Psychology, 11*(2), 95–11.

Salzman, M. (2001). Cultural trauma and recovery: Perspectives from terror management theory. *Trauma, Violence & Abuse: A Review Journal,* 2(2), 172–191. https://doi.org/10.1177/1524838001002002005.

Salzman, M. (2005). The dynamics of cultural trauma: Implications for the pacific nations. In A. J. Marsella, A. Austin, & B. Grant (Eds.), *Social change and psychosocial adaptation in the Pacific Islands: Cultures in transition* (pp. 29–52). New York, NY: Springer.

Salzman, M. B., & Halloran, M. J. (2004). Cultural trauma and recovery: Cultural meaning, self-esteem, and the re-construction of the cultural anxiety-buffer. In J. Greenberg, S. L. Koole, & T. Pyszczynski (Eds.), *Handbook of experimental existential psychology* (pp. 231–246). New York: Guilford.

Solomon, S., Greenberg, J., & Pyszcyznski, T. (1991). A terror management theory of social behavior: The psychological functions of self-esteem and cultural worldviews. In M. P. Zanna (Ed.), *Advances in experimental social psychology* (pp. 91–159). San Diego: Academic Press.

Stannard, D. E. (1989). *Before the horror*. Honolulu: University of Hawai'i Social Science Research Institute.

Stanner, W. E. H. (1979). *White man got no dreaming*. Canberra, Australia: Australian National University Press.

Val, B. V. (1994). The passage out. In K. R. Howe, R. C. Kiste, & B. V. Val (Eds.), *The tides of history: The Pacific islands in the twentieth century* (pp. 435–461). Honolulu, HI: University Press.

Wessels, M. G., & Bretherton, D. (2000). Psychological reconciliation: National and international perspectives. *Australian Psychologist, 35*, 109–117.

Zunin, I. (2014, June 14). Cultural reawakening brings Marquesas back from the brink. *Honolulu Star Advertiser*, p. B6.

Chapter 7
Historical Narratives: Stories We Live By

Distant Time Stories
Historical narratives
Heroic narratives
Narratives (stories) as a source of meaning

7.1 Narratives

The need for intercultural understanding in a world plagued by intercultural conflict is compelling and profound. Intercultural understanding is a necessary foundation for world peace. The "victors" of conflicts between groups and nations usually write history but the experience of significant and traumatic events is transmitted through generations via family narratives and cultural values. Hofstede (2003) suggested that one cannot understand a peoples' culture without understanding their history. The need for intercultural understanding in a world plagued by intercultural conflict is compelling and profound. The purpose of this inquiry is to examine how intercultural understanding may be enhanced through an understanding of peoples' history and historical narratives. Historical narratives influence how people see the world and their place in it and the behaviors needed to guide them safely and successfully through it. Numerous scholars (i.e., Shank & Abelson, 1995) have proposed that virtually all human knowledge is based on stories constructed around past experiences. New experiences are interpreted in terms of old stories. The content of story memories depends on whether and how they are told to others, and these reconstituted memories form the basis of the individual's (and communities) remembered self. Stories about experiences and the experiences of others are the fundamental constituents of human memory, knowledge and communication. The experience of significant and traumatic events is transmitted across generations via narratives. These are stories embedded with meaning and explanation. Meaning is an essential human need because we seek and require meaning to maintain a sense of psychological equanimity in the face of

M.B. Salzman, *A Psychology of Culture*, International and Cultural Psychology,
https://doi.org/10.1007/978-3-319-69420-7_7

the demands of life in an existentially threatening human condition. Narratives are vehicles of meaning. Humans act on the basis of the meaning they attribute to behaviors, situations and events. Therefore, a careful and empathetic (non-judgmental) listening to the narratives of those with who we are in conflict is an essential component of intercultural understanding and world peace.

Liu et al. (2009) assessed social representations of world history among university samples in 12 different and diverse countries including China, Russia, Brazil, Hungary and Spain. Their findings confirmed that, across cultures, transcending boundaries of political ideology, or civilization age world history is represented as a story about politics and warfare. History itself is recognized across the social sciences and by politicians as an important symbolic resource to be mobilized in arguments particularly in support of nationalism. They, consistent with TMT and Social Identity Theory, they assert that a central element in most forms of nationalism is an emphasis of the immortality of the group through time. The immortality strivings identified by TMT are then addressed by group identification supported by historical narratives and a personal identification with such narratives. History is encoded as a story.

Intercultural understanding is a necessary foundation for world peace. One cannot understand a people's culture without understanding their history (Hofstede, 2003). The "victors" of conflicts between groups and nations usually write history but the experience of significant and traumatic events is transmitted through generations via family narratives and cultural values. A peoples' history is often buried but remain potent in the way a people view the world, their place in it and the behaviors needed to guide them safely, securely and successful through their lives in the world as they understand it. All cultures seem to have master narratives or stories related to traumatic (or "heroic") events in their history.

Past humiliations and traumatic experiences resonate in current inter-group relations through the power of the narratives that describe them. Worldview shaping events affecting current realities occur among all peoples, nations and cultures. The imperialistic subjugation and perceived humiliation of China in the 1800s following the Opium War and the conflicting historical narratives of Palestinians and Israelis concerning the founding of Israel are examples of old stories imposed on new situations. All peoples have their stories and they often conflict with the stories of others in the meanings attributed to significant events. The Palestinian historical narrative of a humiliating catastrophe (Nakba) of displacement by the founding of Israel directly conflicts with the Israeli redemptive narrative for the need to return "home" and for safety, recovery, and security in a dangerous and threatening world made salient by the Holocaust. In Hawai'i, the recovery of a buried history has energized a post-colonial narrative that has motivated a cultural renaissance as well as political sovereignty movements that have contributed to a psychological process of decolonization (Salzman, 2005).

In numerous conflict s around the world (i.e., Kosovo and the Balkans) past insecurities, perceptions of humiliations and grievance fuel conflict and confound the possibilities of peace and intercultural understanding. Mutual understanding is an essential component of conflict resolution and the construction of peace. People need to listen to each other and through empathetic listening understanding may be achieved.

Empathetic understanding of the stories of those we are in conflict with does not imply agreement or endorsement of those narratives but just a non-judgmental comprehension of history as viewed through the perspectives of another people. This must be an act of intention because truly listening for empathetic understanding is not a naturally act for most humans. This is particularly true under conditions of conflict and mortality salience (Greenberg, Solomon, & Pyszczynski, 1997). This chapter will examine the role of history and its varied interpretations in the current relations among peoples in conflict and their implications for the construction of peace through intercultural understanding.

7.2 So What's Your Story?

When the street scholars of the author's Brooklyn neighborhood were confronted by seemingly inexplicable behavior or phenomena they would say…. "What's Your Story?" Did the street scholars of Brooklyn somehow realize that inexplicable behavior may be understandable if the personal, cultural, and/or historical narrative of the actor(s) is revealed? In a particular case the street scholars, who worshipped the legendary Brooklyn Dodger baseball team were astounded by a neighborhood character who wore the baseball cap of a rival team from Cincinnati. The street scholars referred to the character as "Cincy" and never really called him by any other name. They demanded, "So what's your story?" Cincy never revealed his story that may have explained the seemingly blasphemous behavior and this neighborhood phenomenon remained inexplicable.

7.3 The Contributions of Narrative Psychology

Shank and Abelson (1995) proposed that virtually all human knowledge is based on stories constructed around past experiences and that new experiences are interpreted in terms of old stories. The content of story memories depends on whether and how they are told to others and these reconstituted memories form the basis of an individuals' or communities' remembered self. The stories about experiences and the experiences of others, then, are the fundamental constituents of human memory, knowledge, communication, meaning and therefore …behavior. People have, for thousands of years been telling stories to each other as they try to comprehend what is going on around them by referring to what they already know in order to make sense of new input. People produce, tell, and repeat master narratives that have profound cultural relevance. The Passover story, the Easter story, the story of the Crusades and the multitude of the world's creation stories are told and retold over the years and offer an interpretive reference point to understand current experience. These master narratives that often reflect truly traumatic events in the life of a people, fuel and maintain existing conflicts as peoples use conflicting narratives to explain their experience of current events. Bridging or integrating conflicting historical narratives may support the alleviation of what are often ferocious, zero-sum, and seemingly intractable conflicts. Stories are flexible, easily indexed and can help interpret a variety of new circumstances. Perhaps most importantly for peace making, narratives can be jointly constructed to include the essential perspectives of each party in a conflict rather excluding the possibility of empathic understanding and reconciliation.

Narrative psychology is premised on the assumption that human experience and behavior are meaningful and that in order to understand ourselves and others, we need to explore the meaning systems and the structures of meaning that construct our minds and our subjective realities (Polkinghorne, 1988). The basic principle, then, is that individuals understand themselves through the medium of language, through talking and writing and that is through these processes that individuals are constantly engaged in the process of defining and creating themselves. This holds true for communities of people as well as individuals. Ultimately, this relates to the core human need for meaning and the essential function of culture as a meaning system that renders the human experience explicable. The construction and transmission of meaning may be accomplished through the telling and hearing of cultural and historical narratives that reverberate across generations that become the interpretative references for new experiences. New experiences are interpreted in terms of old stories and new conflicts may arise through the superimposition of old stories on new events. When we seek the meaning of an experience or observation we are asking ourselves (or others) how something is related or connected to something or something we think we know. The connections or relationship among events constitute their meaning. These meanings are formulated through cultural meaning systems such as language (and narratives) that reverberate with knowledge of connections and relationships across generations. Narratives about one's experiences and the experiences of others are the fundamental constituents of human memory, knowledge, and social communication (Crossely, 2000). This argument essentially proposes that:

- Virtually all human knowledge is based on stories constructed around past experiences.
- New experiences are interpreted in terms of old stories.
- The content of story memories depends on whether and how they are told to others and these reconstituted memories form the basis of the individual's remembered self.

7.4 Features and Characteristics of Narratives

Humans are meaning seeking and meaning needing organisms (Salzman, 2008). Bruner (1991) described ten features of narrative that contribute to this instrument of mind that serves the essential functions of constructing reality and imbuing life experiences with meaning. A brief description of common features and characteristics of narratives follow. They are:

- Narrative diachronicity: A narrative is an account of events occurring over time.
- Particularity: Narratives take as their reference particular happenings. These happenings are representative of broader types.
- Intentional State Entailment: Narratives are about people acting in a setting and the happenings that befall them are relevant to their intentional states while so engaged. These intentional states are relevant to the actors' beliefs, values, theories or desires.
- Hermeneutic composability: The telling of a story and its comprehension as a story depend on the human capacity to process knowledge in an interpretive way. Events need to be constituted as a story in order to enhance their interpretability. The act of constructing a narrative is more than selecting events from memory or history and then placing them in the appropriate order. The events need to be constituted in the light of the overall narrative and made functions of the story.
- Canonicity and Breach: Narratives require but are more than cultural scripts that define how one is supposed to act and be in certain culturally defined situations. A narrative "worth telling" needs to be about how an implicit canonical script has been breached; violated or deviated from in a way that does violence to the very "legitimacy" of the canonical script (i.e., "the betrayed wife").
- Referentiality: Narrative "truth" is judged by the appearance or semblance of being true or real rather than its verifiability. Events and expressions within the narrative are never free from the narrative as a whole.
- Genericness: There are recognizable kinds or genres of narratives such as tragedy, humiliation, and farce. These genres may serve to represent conventionalized human plights that achieve their effects by using language in a particular way ….a way of telling the story. Narrative genre, then is not only a way of constructing human plights but a means through which the mind is guided by the use of "enabling language (p. 15)"
- Normativeness: Bruner (1991) proposes that narratives are essentially normative and that this "normativeness" is not historically or culturally terminal or fixed as they change with the preoccupations of the times and the circumstances surrounding their productions. Therefore, stories can change in their construction and interpretation.
- Context sensitivity and negotiability: We assimilate attribute meaning to narratives by taking the teller's intentions into account in terms of our own background knowledge or prejudices. This context sensitivity makes narrative discourse a viable instrument for cultural negotiation where each party tells their versions in an effort to negotiate meanings.
- Narrative accrual: The accrual of narratives constructs tradition, history and culture. Bruner (1991) argues that one of the principle ways in which we can work in common is by the process of joint narrative accrual. Of course in order to do this we must listen empathically. Empathetic listening, as we shall see, does not imply agreement or judgment just hearing and understanding the stories of the others with whom we may be in conflict. So cultures may be seen as an accrual of narratives and the meanings they imply.

7.5 Culture and the Stories We Live By

Human beings seek meaning and culture infuses the world with meaning (Salzman, 2008). A culture can be thought of as a community of individuals who see their world in a particular manner and who share particular interpretations central to the meaning of their lives and actions. The young learn to tell the dominant stories of their cultural groups whether they are scientific, historical, moral, religious, political or racial. Cultural differences might, then, be rooted in the preferred stories used by different groups of people sharing the same meanings and interpretations of their histories, victories, struggles, humiliations, and aspirations (Howard, 1991). These are cultural narratives. When narratives of contending groups of people differ they may fuel and maintain seemingly intractable conflicts by motivating cognitions (Jost, 2006) that support existing and self-serving attributions.

People seek to make sense of complex emotion-laden events. We often do this reflexively in terms of old stories in a manner that offers simple explanations that serve to reinforce stereotypes, justifying a positive and sympathetic image of oneself or one's group while de-legitimizing, dehumanizing or even demonizing the "other." Such psycho-cultural narratives offer an explanatory framework that contains powerful images and judgments about the motivations and actions of one's own group (i.e., pure, honorable and good) and the "other" (i.e., murderous, barbaric, evil). These narratives may be especially potent in times of uncertainty, anxiety and the awareness of mortality (Pyszczynski et al., 2006). Seeing oneself as playing a part in an epic narrative of a triumph over "evil" (e.g., the crusades, jihad) is psychologically seductive to anxiety prone creatures (human beings) who seek symbolic immortality in the face of an existential dilemma. This uniquely human dilemma is the result of the contradiction between an awareness of the inevitability of mortality (and its attendant physical annihilation) and the universal biological motive of striving for life and continued existence (Becker, 1975; Pyszczynski, Motyl, & Abdollahi, 2009).

Narratives and their metaphors reveal a great deal about how individuals and groups understand the perceived social and political realities they inhabit and reveal deep fears and perceived threats that may fuel defensive responses that provoke and nourish conflict (Ross, 2001). Perceptions of denigration and humiliation are extremely potent and motivating factors that while rooted in history are easily triggered "old stories" that are superimposed on current realities. Such superimposition contains the real possibility of error and produce horrible consequences. The Chinese historical narrative of the humiliation of the Opium War and its consequences remains a potent factor influencing China's perception and behavior toward the West today. Jihadists invoke their narrative of the Crusades and the Crusaders to justify Holy War. When the Ayatollah Ali Kamenei used his speech at a Friday Prayer in Tehran to denounce Britain as the most evil of Iran's enemies he was striking deep historical resonance in the Iranian narrative of the long history of British imperialistic intrusions, insult and humiliations of the nation and its culture. The ease in which such narratives may be evoked can mobilize masses of people (Burns, 2009).

Russia's long history, for example, includes numerous invasions across her borders. This history has generated potent narratives that motivate strong reactions to any appearance of encirclement or threat on her borders. Pipes (2009), a former cold warrior, recommends that the West be exceedingly careful in avoiding any measures that would convey the impression that we are trying militarily to "encircle" the Russian Federation.

The response to perceived threat is a common motivation for destructive behavior. It is therefore essential that we seek an understanding of the central and foundational narratives of peoples with whom we interact and seek to reduce the likelihood of conflict due to an activation of historical narratives relating to experiences of threat, denigration and humiliation. A people and nations contain multiple stories of their history and relations with others. A knowledge of a peoples available narratives may inform behaviors that activate narratives that reduce defensiveness and enhance the possibilities of peace through intercultural understanding and empathy. The creation of new narratives emphasizing mutual respect and cooperation may assist the construction of peace and beneficial relations among peoples.

Rotberg (2006) describes how narratives may justify and maintain conflict. A narrative of grievance, accusation, humiliation and indignity justifies every conflict. Conflicts depend on narratives, and in some senses cannot exist without a detailed explanation of how and why the battles began, and why one side, and only one side, is in the right. Narratives also create conflict, or at least lead directly into clashes. Stories are stitched together into an all-encompassing narrative that becomes available when hostilities loom between opposing camps, polities, and nations. "The texture of the narrative partly determines the contours of a conflict. Thus, conflicts cannot easily start, be consummated, or be resolved without an awareness and attention to the narratives of both sides to conflicts (p. vii)."

7.6 The Role of Narratives in the Production and Maintenance of Conflict

The core of narratives of struggle, humiliation, victory and defeat constitute collective memory. This memory may not be "true" but portrays "truths" that are func tional and consistent with perceived interests and goals. Such collective memories are biased, selective and distorted, They are what Jost (2006) called "motivated cognitions." Every conflict is justified by a narrative of grievance, accusation, indignity and humiliation. Such conflict supporting narratives contain assumptions that become self-fulfilling justifications that may justify violence to achieve noble ends, serve as instruments of motivation, bolster stereotypes and serve to demonize or dehumanize the "other" while attributing only the most noble and justifiable motives to oneself or group (Rotberg, 2006). Ross (2001) poses these relevant questions:

How do people make sense of complex, emotional-laden events?

Why do different, seemingly contradictory accounts of the same event develop and co-exist?
How do we make meaning of conflict?

7.7 "Intractable Conflicts" and the Narratives That Support Them

Intractable conflicts are those that are protracted, seemingly irreconcilable, violent, of a zero-sum nature and promote a major expenditure of time and resources by the parties in conflict. Narratives supporting intractable conflicts have major consequences for information processing as we impose old stories onto new information thereby nourishing and maintaining the conflict. Narratives of collective memories relating to an intractable conflict provide an unambiguous black-and-white picture that enables a parsimonious, unequivocal, and simple understanding of the history of the conflict. Information is selectively received, encoded and interpreted according to the narrative's schemata thus limiting the extent to which beliefs about the "other" can be influenced by new perceptions. In-group members expect the worst from the "other" thereby producing behaviors that nourish a self-fulfilling and increasing cycle of conflict. The narratives associated with intractable conflicts, therefore, close minds and prolong the conflict (Bar-Tal & Salomon, 2006).

The narrative of collective memory touches important themes that influence the perception of the conflict and its maintenance. The narrative justifies the outbreak of the conflict and the course of its development. It outlines the reasons for the supreme and existential importance of the conflicting goals, stressing that failure to achieve them may threaten the very existence of the group. The narrative of collective memory disregards the goals of the other side by describing them as unjustified, unreasonable or the product of inferior or "evil" beings. Empirical research has supported hypotheses, generated from Terror Management Theory (TMT), predicting that under conditions of mortality salience, a common condition in such conflicts, people tend to bolster their cultural worldviews and to derogate, distance themselves and even aggress against the different "other" (Greenberg et al., 1997).

It is difficult to conceive of an intractable conflict that is not supported by competing narratives. In Hawai'i, preparations for an official statehood celebration, with a supporting narrative of justification, included the "lei-bedecked arrival of the USS Hawai'i, a $2.5 billion nuclear submarine billed by the Honolulu Star Bulletin as 7700 tons of Aloha" (Conrow, 2009). A conflicting narrative of how and why Hawai'i became part of the United States counters the narrative supporting this celebration. This narrative describes an illegal overthrow of the independent Hawaiian Nation that was supported by prevailing attitudes of white supremacy that enabled the annexation of an independent and sovereign nation. Conrow (2009) cites Saranillo, "Colonization or occupation isn't just about dominating another people. You dominate those people by not letting them tell their history, not letting them speak their experiences, not letting them express themselves as a people. Colonization tries to interpret and block that and speak on behalf of those people" (p. 4). The story(ies) of the colonized and oppressed may break through the dominant/colonial story explosively. A peoples' story seeks expression. An unheard story demands to be heard.

In Xinjiang, China the Uighur people protest and rebel against the Han Chinese who arrived in large numbers after the 1949 revolution. In the Uighur narrative the Han are seen as colonizers and oppressors in their ancestral homeland whereas the Han narrative describes the conflict as resulting from an ungrateful minority that does not appreciate the economic development they brought to Xinjiang which is seen as an inalienable part of China that always held sway over the territory that lies at the crossroads of Asian civilizations.

Similarly, the conflict between Tibetans and the Chinese government is supported by conflicting narratives that reveal a "deep, emotional chasm between the way many Chinese and Tibetans view their recent shared history" (Wong, 2009). The iconic image of smiling Tibetans raising a giant portrait of Chairman Mao as they walk under a clear blue sky reflects the Chinese government's narrative that its rule over Tibet brought hope and development to a poor, isolated and feudal land while many Tibetans read this relationship as a tragic end to their independence. The Tibetans' story describes their traditional homeland as the exclusive territory of the Tibetan people whereas the Chinese interpret the absence of Chinese authority in Tibet as part of their national humiliation. Humiliation is a searing personal and national experience that requires relief. This relief may take extremely destructive compensatory forms. As stated previously, a narrative of grievance, accusation, indignity and humiliation justifies every conflict and humiliation is a profound human experience that is not easily forgotten or forgiven. The experience of humiliation is a deep dysphoric feeling that is associated the perception of oneself as being unjustly degraded or ridiculed and where one's very identity is demeaned (Hartling & Luchetta, 1999). Such a psychological condition motivates compensatory actions that may relieve this highly aversive state and these actions may be extremely destructive. Memmi (2006) implores us to recognize and realize the sense of profound humiliation and resentment that that inhabits much of the former "third world" and, more specifically the Arab world. He suggests "this is the resentment of the conquered who see no obvious outlet for their defeat" (p. 94). When one is beaten down and humiliated by defeat few alternatives seem to be available except to dream of a "nostalgic past when one was powerful and rich, wise and cultivated with mythical ancestors, superhuman heroes, kings ruling over vast empires" (p. 95). This is a narrative of a glorious future when one will be, once again be rich and prosperous and invincible. Jihadists are explicit in their intention to re-establish a Caliphate that extends its dominion over vast territories and populations.

Narratives of humiliation, victimization and compensatory redemption fuel current violent Middle Eastern conflicts where participants are unlikely to ask themselves what their contribution to the conflict might be. An awareness of one's contribution to a conflict, particularly one in which blood has been shed, requires an act of intentional empathy. It requires a willingness to hear the story of the "other" while judgment is withheld and an understanding of the complexity of the conflict and the contributions of all parties is sought. Each party must acknowledge what is valid in the competing narrative and its own contributions to the problem. The Palestinian–Israeli conflict may well be an exemplar of an "intractable conflict" described earlier. Conflict resolution depends on changes in the collective narratives of the parties involved. Part of this process involves seeking and learning about the rival group's collective memories supporting the historical narrative. An acknowledgment of the past implies recognition that there are indeed two narratives that are at least partially valid from the point of view of the "other" (Bar-Tal & Salomon, 2006). It is problematic that intractable conflicts nourished by the flow of blood make this very difficult to accomplish.

7.8 The Need for Cultural Empathy

The necessary task of seeking an empathetic understanding of the position of the "other" must of necessity be an act of intention. Van Der Zee and Van Oudenhoven (2000) identified cultural empathy as one of the five factors assessed by their instrument designed to assess multicultural effectiveness. Their cultural empathy scale assesses the capacity to identify with the feelings, thoughts and behavior of individuals from different cultural backgrounds. Ba-Isa (2008), writing in Arab News, states that the goal of cross-cultural understanding must be a realistic cultural empathy that requires oneself to inhabit the psychological shoes of another and describe behavior objectively rather than evaluatively. He writes that it is impossible to understand a behavior unless the behavior is described objectively and that realistic cultural empathy is not sympathy, agreement or identification with the "other" and his or her culture. Realistic cultural empathy is the intellectual understanding of a culture's values and beliefs. Such an understanding makes it more likely that the reactions of people to given situations (i.e., perceived violations of "honor") may be accurately predicted and that deadly consequences may be averted. Cultural empathy has also been described and prescribed in the counseling profession as "seeing the world through another's eyes, hearing as they might hear, and feeling and experiencing their internal world" (Ivey, Ivey, & Simek-Morgan, 1993, p. 21). Empathetic understanding does not imply agreement or disagreement, approval or disapproval but only an understanding and a communication of that understanding. Realistic cultural empathy also has the capacity to enhance one's awareness of one's own values, beliefs and identity. However, when immersed in the dynamics of conflict where the "other" is dehumanized as the incarnation of evil the intentional practice cultural empathy may be as unappealing as it is necessary for the resolution of intractable conflicts and the competing narratives that support them.

7.9 What Is to Be Done? Reconciling Conflicting and Competing Narratives

As previously stated, all conflicts seem to be justified by narratives of grievance, humiliation, indignity, injustice or existential danger. Rotberg (2006) suggests that the first step is to know and truly hear the competing narratives. Secondly, to the extent possible efforts must be made to reconcile or bridge the conflicting narratives. This process requires that each side find elements in the competing narrative that can be respected and seen as valid. This is obviously not an easy process since the different sides tell vastly different stories, and the act of preserving them is, in essence, a political and psychological statement that embodies the hopes, fears, grievances and hurts experienced over time in the history of the intractable conflict. Perhaps no conflict better expresses the difficulties of reconciling conflicting narratives than the Palestinian—Israeli conflict and no battle over the regional historic record is more contested than the one over the story of Israel's establishment. The narrative surrounding and explaining the founding and defense of the State of Israel is seen, by Israel's as the historic return home and redemption of the Jewish people whereas for the Palestinian narrative describes the founding of Israel as a catastrophe or the "Nakba."

Conflicting and Competing Narratives and the Palestinian—Israeli Conflict: Some years ago the author attended the belated Bat Mitzvah (a Jewish rite of passage) of his sister-in-law. The Rabbi seemed to summarize the essence of the Jewish historical narrative in a brief statement "our enemies tried to destroy us and we survived." As previously indicated, the perspective of narrative psychology indicates that we interpret new situations in terms of old stories. The author wondered if the current realities of Israeli-Palestinian conflict are distorted by the imposition of this essential Jewish historical narrative that may produce a self-fulfilling prophecy.

Ross (2001) describes explanatory, conflict nourishing "psycho-cultural" narratives as simple accounts (stories) that contain powerful images and judgments about the motivations and actions of one's own group and the "others." These stories are emotionally significant for individuals and groups. People seek meaning and understanding of their worlds and the anxiety producing events that transpire in their lives. Narratives address these needs as people struggle to make sense of these events. The founding of the State of Israel has produced two very different narratives that explain the experiences of two peoples in conflict. The meaning of "Nakba" is "castrophe." The joyful "return" of the Jewish people to their ancient homeland was a castrophe for the people who were displaced by the founding of the State of Israel. These competing narratives may be considered as part of the cultural worldviews of the two peoples in conflict in a small land. TMT (see Greenberg et al., 1997) researchers have shown that under conditions of mortality salience (e.g., war and its consequent bloodshed) tend to bolster existing worldviews and the narratives they contain. As minds close and the "other" are derogated, demonized and dehumanized murderous acts are justified and further conflict is nourished. Can these conflicting narratives be bridged and a new narrative created that contains essential elements of each side's "story?" For this to occur the question ("What's Your Story?") must be asked with all possible sincerity, intention, and open-ness and the answer to this question must be heard and understood and then communicate that understanding without judgment. People need to be heard and understood as a prerequisite for the construction of a narrative of supportive of reconciliation or at least conflict management. An example of such an effort is a group of Israeli citizens who are working to raise awareness of the "Nakba" (the Palestinian "castrophe" of 1948) among Israelis through an NGO called "Zochrot" ("Remembering").

7.10 Revising and Reconstructing the Narratives of Intractable Conflict

Zochrot describes the Nakba as the destruction of more than 500 Palestinian villages and cities and the expulsion of over 750,000 residents during the war that led to the creation of the State of Israel. The Nakba is seen as the central, unspoken (in Israel) trauma at the core of the Israel/Palestine conflict and the telling of this story is essential for achieving reconciliation between the peoples of that land (Hirschfield, 2007). Zochrot's intention is to bring the story of the Nakba to the Jewish-Israeli people and to integrate that story with "our story." For those willing to listen past the pain, fear, and self justifications—this would be an act of intentional cultural empathy.

Bar-On (2006) suggests three strategies of narrative reconstruction and revision that seems prerequisite to peace and reconciliation:

- Uncover and peel off the prevailing narrative's exclusionist, nationalistic and self-congratulatory ideologies that tend to distort the narrative.
- Transcend simplistic generalizations and labeling, and discover the full complexity of the disputed events both their motives and causations.
- Try to understand the motives and rationale of the "other's" behavior, and to present the narrative with maximum sensitivity to the sensibilities of the opposite side, with human compassion and a deeper understanding of the tragic nature of the conflict.

Price (2007) describes a potentially transformative process of narrative mediation that accompanied the transition of South Africa from an apartheid state to a multi-racial, multi-cultural democracy based on equality and respect. This transformation resulted in a new story of a new South Africa that attempted to confer a larger superordinate identity to its citizens. Given the indignities and humiliations suffered by a majority of the population at the hands of an apartheid system it is remarkable that this transformation has occurred without significant bloodshed. The process involves the integration of narratives within a mediation process that includes restorative justice processes designed to produce a fundamental transformation of the very fabric of South African society. Key to this approach is a mutual recognition that the conflict may not have to be addressed directly but indirectly by investigating and acknowledging (empathically) the meanings each give to the conflict and what a more preferred relationship might look like. In this sense the unproductive question of who is right or wrong becomes a question of how to construct a joint narrative with solutions that may point to a better future. This narrative mediation elevates a persons (or a peoples') own understanding of the story over the "facts." The pursuit of "truth" in this process is less important than how stories construct reality and how peoples in conflict may construct a preferred story of relationships that is in accord with their values, beliefs, commitments and vital interests. The act of telling a story and being listened to offers a way to process painful memories and experiences while nourishing the courage that is essential to confront each other's pain. Discourses of entitlement informing narratives pose obstacles to this process that must be deconstructed deemphasized, and integrated into a new "we" narrative. These entitlement discourses include "manifest destiny," "American exceptionalism," and various justification stories about divine rights and privileges to land and resources. These entitlements present formidable barriers to narrative mediation and reconciliation.

Ross (2001) suggests that narratives supporting intractable conflicts are complex and that the first step in reconciliation, following the telling and hearing of the conflicting narratives, is finding ways to identify and emphasize common concerns and seek possible congruence. He proposes that a psycho-cultural change strategy requires the introduction of new experiences that invite the construction of new meanings attributed to events described in the narratives. Ross suggests that a reconciliation of competing narratives requires:

- Better listening and understanding of the competing narrative and the pain, hurt, and humiliations suffered by the "other"
- Acknowledgement that is based on empathic understanding of the hurts and threats perceived and experienced by the "other."
- The development of new policies and actions.

The challenge, then, is to transform hateful, self-justifying single narratives into mutually inclusive, respectful and sensitive "stories." Clearly this is not easy, especially once blood has been spilled (mortality salience). Such an effort must be an act of intention informed by the horror of intractable conflict and the possibility of constructing a better future. So when it is most difficult to do so we must ask the question of ourselves and of the "other" with who we are in conflict:

What's your story?
What's my story?
What's OUR story?

The street corner philosophers of the author's Brooklyn neighborhood may have had a point.

References

Ba-Isa, M.Y. (2008, June 6). Cultural empathy doesn't need your sympathy. *Arab News*.

Bar-Tal, D., & Salomon, G. (2006). Israeli-jewish narratives of the israeli-palestinian conflict. In R. I. Rotberg (Ed.), *Israeli and palestinian narratives of conflict: History's double helix*. Bloomington, IN: Indiana University Press.

Becker, E. (1975). *Escape from evil*. New York: Free Press.

Bruner, J. (1991). The narrative construction of reality. *Critical Inquiry, 18*(1), 1–21.

Burns, J.F. (2009, June 20). Ayatollah, calling Britain enemy no. 1, taps into deep distrust rooted in history. *The New York Times*, p. A7.

Conrow, J. (2009, August 12–18). Another side of statehood. *Honolulu Weekly*.

Crossely, M. L. (2000). *Introducing narrative psychology: Self, trauma and the construction of meaning*. Buckingham, U.K.: Open University Press.

Greenberg, J., Solomon, S., & Pyszczynski, T. (1997). Terror management theory of self-esteem and cultural world views: Empirical assessments and conceptual refinements. In M. P. Zanna (Ed.), *Advances in experimental social psychology* (pp. 61–139). San Diego, CA: Academic.

Hartling, L. M., & Luchetta, T. (1999). Humiliation: Assessing the impact of derision, degradation and debasement. *The Journal of Primary Prevention, 19*(4), 259–278.

Hirschfield, R. (2007, May 1). Norma Musih, Zochrot and the Nakba. *Washington Report on Middle East Affairs*. Washington, DC.

Hofstede, G. (2003). *Culture's consequences, comparing values, behaviors, institutions, and organizations across nations* (2nd ed.). Beverly Hills, CA: Sage.

Howard, G. (1991). Culture tales. *American Psychologist, 47*(3), 187–197.

Ivey, A., Ivey, M., & Simek-Morgan, L. (1993). *Counseling and psychotherapy: A multicultural perspective* (3rd ed.). Boston: Allyn & Bacon.

Jost, J. T. (2006). The end of the end of ideology. *American Psychologist, 61*, 651–670.

Memmi, A. (2006). *Decolonization and the decolonized*. Minneapolis: University of Minnesota Press.

Liu, J. H., Paez, D., Slawuta, P., Cabecinhas, R., Techio, E., Kokdemir, D., Sen, R., Vincze, O., Muluk, H., Wang, F., & Zlobina, A. (2009). Representing world history in the 21st century: The impact of 9/11, the Iraq war, and the nation-state on dynamics of collective remembering. *Journal of Cross-Cultural Psychology, 4*(40), 667–692.

Pipes, R. (2009, August 24). Pride and power. *The Wall Street Journal*, p. A1.

Price, L. (2007). Narrative mediation: A transformative approach to conflict resolution. *African Initiative for Mediation*.

Pyszczynski, T., Abdollahi, A., Solomon, S., Greenberg, J., Cohen, F., & Weise, D. (2006). Mortality salience, martyrdom, and military might: The Great Satan versus the axis of evil. *Personality and Social Psychology Bulletin, 32*, 525–537.

Pyszczynski, T., Motyl, M., & Abdollahi, A. (2009). Righteous violence: Killing for god, country, freedom, and justice. *Interdisciplinary Research on Terrorism and Political Violence, 1*, 13–40.

Polkinghorne, D. E. (1988). *Narrative knowing and the human sciences*. Albany: State University of New York Press.

Ross, M. H. (2001). *The political psychology of competing narratives: September 11 and beyond*. Brooklyn, NY: The Social Science Research Council.

Rotberg, R. I. (Ed.). (2006). *Israeli and Palestinian Narratives of conflict: History's double helix*. Bloomington, IN: Indiana University Press.

Salzman, M. (2005). Contextualizing the symptom in multicultural consultation: Anger in the family a cultural-historical context. *Journal of Educational and Psychological Consultation, 16*(3), 223–237.

Salzman, M. B. (2008). Globalization, religious fundamentalism and the need for meaning. *International Journal of Intercultural Relations, 32*(4), 318–327.

Shank, R. C., & Abelson, R. P. (1995). Knowledge and memory: The real story. In R. S. Wyer Jr. (Ed.), *Advances in social cognition* (Vol. VIII, pp. 1–86). Hillsdale, NJ: Lawrence Erlbaum Associates.

Van Der Zee, K. I., & Van Oudenhoven, J. P. (2000). The multicultural personality questionnaire: A multidimensional instrument of multicultural effectiveness. *European Journal of Personality, 14*, 291–309.

Wong, G. (2009, March 13). Tibet: 2 sides see history differently. *Honolulu Star Bulletin*, p. 2.

Chapter 8
Intercultural and Inter-group Relations

Ethno-cultural conflict and cooperation
Sources of conflict
Cultures and conflict
Cultural threat: What's at stake?
Conditions of prejudice reduction
Constructing situations that optimize the potential for positive intercultural interaction
Mutual respect
Cultural Empathy

The issue of intercultural relations and their potentials is of vital importance. These potentials range from mutual enrichment and cooperation to murderous conflict. Given the perspective of culture offered in this book and the psychological and adaptive functions of culture, this is not surprising. Huntington (1996) predicted "In this new, globalized, world the most pervasive, important and dangerous conflicts will not be between social classes, the rich and the poor, or other economically defined groups, but between peoples belonging to different cultural entities" (p. 28). Marsella (2005) assessed that "The lesson from past and present conflicts is that "culture" is a critical determinant of conflict and every consideration must be given to cultural factors in understanding the origins, escalation, resolution and prevention of conflict" (p. 653). Why might this be so? He suggested, as referenced earlier, the following pathways to intercultural conflict and violence:

- Perception of -danger to national or group survival, identity, well-being;
- Perception of the "other" as evil dangerous, threatening;
- Perception of situation as unjust, unequal, unfair, humiliating, punishing;
- Perception of self as self-righteous, moral, justified, and "good" by virtue of religion, history, identity (e.g., "American Exceptionalism"). Considering the vital psychological functions of culture can culturally diverse peoples co-exist in mutually enriching ways rather than killing each other in bloody conflicts based on alternative constructions of reality.

M.B. Salzman, *A Psychology of Culture*, International and Cultural Psychology,
https://doi.org/10.1007/978-3-319-69420-7_8

As indicated earlier, we humans have a serious existential problem that may fuel inter-cultural conflict. We have cognitive capacities that seem unique to humans that lead us to ponder difficult questions for which there are no definitive answers. This is especially true of the question of mortality and our awareness that we will ultimately face physical annihilation and is unable to fulfill the basic biological motive to continue existence (Pyszczynski, Greenberg, & Solomon, 1997). We possess an awareness that we are born into and most certainly die in an uncontrollable indeterminate universe and this is terrifying to cognitively complex human creatures who are aware in Becker's terms (1971) that we are, physically, ultimately "food for worms." This is an observable fact the meanings of which are beliefs largely derived from culture and religion. This existential problem is universal and observable. How people address this fact varies across cultures. Culturally diverse answers to this essential human problem provide for the potential for conflict especially under conditions of threat (McGregor et al., 1998) and most specifically the condition of "mortality salience." Considering the vital psychological functions of culture can culturally diverse peoples co-exist in mutually enriching ways rather than killing each other in bloody conflicts based on alternative constructions of reality.

Cultures address this existential problem by offering some promise of immortality, literal or symbolic, to those who believe in the cultural worldview and see themselves as living up to its standards. Literal promises of immortality are offered by religious beliefs. Symbolic solutions to the problem may occur by providing for the conviction that one is a valued part of something absolutely meaningful that extends beyond self in time and space. This conviction provides for the possibility of making a contribution or a permanent mark on the world or history by what one produces. This book is the author's humble attempt to identify and describe what he thinks he has learned about culture and its psychological functions and to contribute it to the "life force" and world. Erikson (1959) refers to this motive as "generativity" or the urge to contribute to the next generation and to posterity. We need to feel our lives matter—that we matter. Culture tells us how to "matter" and how to manage the existential terror inherent in human existence.

Ethno-cultural conflict is a global and historic problem (Huntington, 1996). It's a big problem. The causes of ethno-cultural conflict are multiple. Considering the vital psychological functions of culture (Salzman, 2001a, 2001b, 2003) we are challenged to study and consider how culturally diverse peoples can co-exist in mutually enriching ways rather than killing each other in bloody conflicts based on such factors as alternative constructions of reality, competition for material or psychological resources, and efforts to manage anxiety through in-group identification and out-group demonization.

Let's pause to review key implications and inferences derived from hundreds of TMT studies that are relevant to inter-cultural conflict (see Greenberg, Solomon, & Pyszczynski, 1997).

- Culture a psychological defense, cooperatively constructed and maintained to manage the terror (existential anxiety) inherent in the human condition.

- Culture makes self-esteem possible. Self-esteem is a cultural construction. Self-esteem serves as an anxiety buffer. Self-esteem is constructed by having faith in a cultural worldview and seeing oneself as living up to its standards. Self-esteem (however constructed across cultures) serves as an anxiety buffer.
- Cultural conflicts are fueled by numerous factors and conditions and maybe particular vicious due to the psychological stakes involved (competing constructions of reality and immortality strivings).
- TMT experiments have found that when people are made aware of their mortality they bolster and affirm their cultural worldviews, exhibit a strong tendency to like those who support their worldviews while distancing, derogating, and even demonizing those who do not support their cultural worldviews suggesting that culture (and/or religion) offers either literal or symbolic immortality. This may be one reason that wars are so difficulty to stop once blood flows (mortality salience).

Considering the vital psychological functions of culture (Becker, 1971, 1973, 1975; Greenberg, Solomon, & Pyszczynski, 1997) the question that arises is whether culturally diverse peoples can co-exist in mutually enriching ways rather than killing each other in bloody conflicts based on alternative constructions of reality? The issue is of vital importance, in his provocative and influential work Huntington (1996) stated that "In this new world the most pervasive, important and dangerous conflicts will not be between social classes, the rich and the poor, or other economically defined groups, but between peoples belonging to different cultural entities."

Recall that TMT proposes that these varying cultural world-views serve, either literally or symbolically as an "immortality ideology." When different immortality ideologies collide the validity of each is called into question enhancing the possibility of psychological and behavioral defensive reactions that may result in distancing, demonization and attempts to convert "the other" to one's cultural or religious world-view or even the annihilation of those "others." Therefore, from this point of view, the worldview espoused by any given culture is a symbolic social construction that provides a meaningful context in which relatively anxiety free action is possible. Cognitively complex human beings are realistically concerned with their mortality and cultures address this concern. Therefore, culture addresses core human needs. How to deal with the observable fact that we face inevitable physical annihilation is a common human problem answered differently across cultures and immortality ideologies may clash on this vital concern. The anxiety driven need for absolute faith in one's worldview, given the high psychological stakes involved, can produce murderous reactions as well as serve to sustain people through their anxiety prone existence. Historical anti-Semitism provides an example of this dynamic. Goldhagen (1996) cited the religious roots of anti-Semitism by quoting John Chrysostom, "a pivotal church Father." This quote bears repetition as it crystalizes the dilemma of competing immortality ideologies:

> Where Christ-killers gather, the cross is ridiculed, God blasphemed, the father unacknowledged, the son insulted, the grace of Spirit rejected…If the Jewish rites are holy and our way of life must be false. But if our way is true, as indeed it is, theirs is fraudulent. (p. 50)

It seems that human differences on essential existential human concerns provide a context and tendency for intolerance. Which begs the question if must you be wrong for me to be right if we differ on this vital concern? Various models relevant to intercultural conflict have been proposed. They will be briefly summarized below.

8.1 Integrated Threat Theory (Stephan & Stephan (2000))

Stephan and Stephan (2000) hypothesized that prejudice toward ethnic groups may be associate with any or all of four different perceived threats. They are realistic threats, symbolic threats, intergroup anxiety and/or negative stereotypes (see Smith, Bond & Kagitcibasi, p. 231). All four threats are potentially activated when groups come in contact. Realistic threats may include a competition for scarce resources. In such a case conflict is likely but may be transformed through the development of a superordinate goal of expanding the resources (i.e., jobs, food) through equal status collaboration and cooperation. Symbolic threats are central to TMT which proposes that under conditions of existential threat we tend to, in the words of Barack Obama, adhere to our cultural symbols (i.e., guns, flags, faith) and, as evidenced by the American reaction to France after 9/11, derogate those who do not support our position. It is noteworthy that the 9/11 attackers attacked the symbols of American power. By attacking the World Trade Center and the Pentagon they attacked the centers of U.S. military and economic power and symbolic immortality. The result of which produced widespread anxiety, increased church attendance and demands for revenge. Intergroup anxiety is a threat and our responses to anxiety may only exacerbate the issue producing conflict. As Cushner and Brislin (1996) have noted, anxiety is a primary theme in intercultural interactions.

8.2 Realistic Conflict Theory

Realistic Conflict Theory Developed by Sherif (1966) argues that intergroup conflict arises as a result of conflict of interests between groups. For example, when two groups want to achieve the same goal but cannot have it, hostility is produced between them. The theory accounts for intergroup conflict, negative prejudices, and stereotypes as a result of actual competition between groups for desired resources. Sherif found support for his theory in one his most famous experiments, "The Robber's Cave "(Cialdini et al., 1999) that was previously cited. The contentious court decisions related to the claims over the valuable and essential "ceded" lands represents a clear conflict of interest between the State of Hawai'i and the Native Hawaiian people. In addition to their material, spiritual and psychological value this conflict over land is a conflict over an extremely scarce resource.

8.3 The Functionality of Stereotypes

Stereotypes are closely associated with prejudice and discrimination. They pervade people's views of their social worlds. Stereotypes are usually simple, over generalized assertions about what "they" are like. "They" are denied their individuality by having applied to them a set of beliefs about their character and propensities of behavior (Snyder & Miene, 1994). By denying "their" individuality we are ultimately denying their humanity. We see only a category. Dehumanization lies at the root of the indignities and even atrocities that humans impose on fellow humans. What needs are met and psychological functions served by the stereotypes that afflict our social perception and interpersonal behavior? Snyder & Mien describe three orientations associated with three particular functions served by stereotypes.

The *cognitive orientation* assumes that humans are limited in the amount of incoming information they can process, and form stereotypes as one way to reduce the cognitive burden of dealing with a complex world. In this orientation, stereotypes serve the function of *cognitive economy* by reducing incoming data to a man ageable level so as to imbue our worlds with a sense of predictability.

The *psychodynamic orientation* sees stereotypes as providing a variety of ego-defensive functions. They include the derogation of others (particularly those seen as competitors for scarce resources) and the building of self-esteem by engaging in downward social comparison. Stereotypes therefore are subjectively useful for making people feel better about themselves and less threatened by other groups of people. Therefore, in functional terms stereotypes serve the function of ego defense and protection.

The *sociocultural orientation* suggests that stereotypes serve the social function of fitting in and achieving a sense of belonging which has long been recognized as a human need (e.g., Maslow, 1987). Sherif, Harvey, White, Hood, and Sherif (1954) saw such stereotypes as functionally related to becoming a group member thereby serving a social function.

These three types of functions serve real human needs and humans are motivated to satisfy their needs as they are perceived (i.e., the need for a predictable world, the need for self-esteem, and the need to belong). Given their ubiquity and nature, stereotypes must be considered a source of error with potentially serious consequences that call for strategies to minimize their negative impact on human and intergroup relations. Pettigrew (1998) described the as the optimal sequence of contact between groups as first, *decategorization*: seeing similarity with the "other"—seeing the "other" as an individual and interaction as an interpersonal not intergroup event; second, *salient categorization* other's group made salient so the "other" seen as representative of their group in some essential way and; third *recategorization* into a larger category such as "working class" or "human race" that is inclusive ("we world") is created that includes all interactants (Hassan, 2004). In this case a person's individuality, culture and universal humanity are acknowledged and the full humanity of the person is acknowledged so no dehumanization occurs and dehumanization is a prerequisite for discrimination, demonization, and atrocity. This formulation does not "deracialize" but acknowledges differences while including them in a larger formulation. An example of this process may be the development of "local culture" in Hawai'i.

8.4 Ifoga and Indigenous Peacemaking: A Cause for Optimism?

Ethno-cultural conflict is a global and historic problem (Huntington, 1996). It's a big problem. The causes of ethno-cultural conflict are multiple. Considering the vital psychological functions of culture (Salzman, 2001a, 2001b, 2003) we are challenged to study and consider how culturally diverse peoples can co-exist in mutually enriching ways rather than killing each other in bloody conflicts based on such factors as alternative constructions of reality, competition for material or psychological resources, and efforts to manage anxiety through in-group identification and out-group demonization. Culture is a critical determinant and mediator of conflict in disputes between individuals, communities, and nations. Culture can be considered both a source of conflict and an essential means of its resolution. All cultures probably have their own methods to resolve and prevent conflict. An impressive example of this is described below.

In a case, reported in the Honolulu Advertiser (January 13, 2008, pp. A1, A14) a potentially explosive situation was averted between a more established (Samoan) immigrant group and more recent immigrants from Micronesia. In the incident a Samoan youth was stabbed in the heart by a Chuukese youth outside of a housing project in the working class community of Kalihi. The potential for revenge attacks was high but averted due to the Micronesian community employing an indigenous Samoan ritual of apology called Ifoga that involves the community of the attacker humbling themselves in ritual apology before the aggrieved. In this case an offering was made and the apology was accepted. There was no revenge. The use, by the Micronesian of an indigenous Samoan ritual of apology with the assistance of pastors from both communities was seen as instrumental in avoiding further conflict and bloodshed. It was an offering of profound apology and deep respect.

Situations have the power to promote intercultural conflict or harmony. Intergroup contact theory and indigenous conflict resolution strategies, such as Ifoga, point to the possibility of conflict avoidance and the development of positive intercultural relations.

8.5 The Power of the Situation and Conditions of Prejudice Reduction

8.5.1 Intergroup Contact Theory

Allport (1954), Pettigrew (1998) and inter-group contact theory suggest a solution. They have identified conditions for optimal intergroup contact. Allport (1954) identified four conditions for optimal inter-group contact and prejudice reduction. They are:

Equal status contact in the situation (implying equal power in the situation)
Common (superordinate goals)
Intergroup Cooperation in achieving common goals
Support of authority and cultural or societal norms for positive intergroup contact
Friendship potential (added later)—intimate not superficial contact

Allport (1954) and Pettigrew (1998) emphasized the condition of *equal status contact in the situation* implying equal power in the situation. We are challenged to construct such situations as inequality pervades social, political and economic life to greater or lesser degrees throughout the world whether between individuals, groups or nations. A colonial situation was imposed on Hawai'i (Laenui, 2000). Notions of inferiority and superiority are embedded in and supported by the colonial situation (Fanon, 1968; Memmi, 1965). Memmi suggested that the colonial situation casts its actors in the roles of the colonizer and the colonized and it is this situation that is definitive. For these roles to change the situation must change.

These conditions of equal status contact, common (superordinate) goals, intergroup cooperation in achieving common goals, support of authority and cultural or societal norms for positive intergroup contact and the potential for developing friendships through intimate not superficial contact may be intentionally constructed in our schools and communities. An example of a cultural norm supportive of these conditions is the Hawaiian value of Aloha. "Aloha" (literally meaning sacred breath includes a spirit of generosity, welcome, kindness and a broad tolerance of differences among people (Salzman 2012). Taken together these known conditions provide a potential roadmap to a multicultural destiny characterized by an appreciation of diversity, mutual respect and shared interests. By promoting equality and mutual respect we work toward the development of the "equal status" contact. By identifying common interests, we can suggest superordinate goals and promote cooperation as a mode to achieve them.

8.6 An Example from Hawai'i: The Construction of an "Interracial Labor Movement" and the Conditions of Prejudice Reduction

The conditions of prejudice reduction and positive intercultural relations as described by Allport (1954) and Pettigrew (1998) may have been operative in the construction of an interracial, intercultural labor movement that succeeded. From disparate ethnicities, status, languages, races and cultures a superordinate "interracial" labor movement and identity coalesced in the 1940s into a working class movement that transformed the conservative, feudal political realities of Hawai'i into what many consider to be the most progressive state in the United States. The pre-war period that was characterized by profound and entrenched racial divisions was displaced by a protracted period of durable "inter-racialism" that continues to this day (Jung, 2006). Jung contends that the construction of this "we" did not negate or deny race (and ethnicity) but "rearticulated" it by constructing a schema and worldview that saw worker's struggle for racial and class justice as "coincident and mutually reinforcing (p. 9)." Factors that may have contributed to this historical development and how this process may be understood psychologically will be considered in the light of relevant theory.

Native Hawaiian and migrant workers mainly from China, Portugal, Japan, and the Philippines were recruited to work on Hawai'i's sugar plantations in overlapping succession from the middle of the nineteenth century. By the end of the nineteenth century Hawai'i had become a colony of the United States ruled by a cohesive oligarchy of *haole* capitalists (the Big Five) who possessed and wielded an enormous concentration of wealth and power (Cooper & Daws, 1985) throughout the first half of the twentieth century. As agricultural laborers the workers endured low wages and terrible working and living conditions on the plantations where they were stratified by race and ethnicity. As indicated, different groups had access to different conditions based on race and ethnicity. These differences in working and living conditions were supported by stereotypical perceptions of relative inferiority to the elite and powerful and the degree of perceived national loyalty and suitability for inclusion and citizenship. This policy was later redefined by a militant labor movement organized by the International Longshoremen's and Warehousemen's Union (ILWU) as a classic divide and conquer tactics that supported the interests of the oligarchy (Big Five).

Labor did protest and strike prior to WWII but did not do so interracially and across ethnicities. There was a "Great Strike" of Japanese workers in 1909, a Filipino worker strike in 1924, and a dual union (Japanese and Filipino) strike in 1920 that were met with organized and obdurate opposition from capital. The collaboration of Japanese and Filipino workers was a collaboration of two ethnically based unions not an integrated interracial movement. The crushing defeat of the 1920 collaboration caused Japanese workers to withdraw from the labor movement for two decades. The cause for the defeat was attributed to a weak coalition between the unions due to *unequal status in the plantation system* and the resulting stereotypical perceptions of each group toward the other. This attempt at collaboration had an unsuccessful outcome.

Environmental and contextual factors influencing plantation labor changed in the 1930s with the passage of the Wagner Act and the arrival of the National Labor Relations Board (NLRB) which facilitated organizing unions and subjected employers to sanctions for the most blatant anti-union actions. There was *authoritative* support, then, for organizing and the development of a labor movement across race and ethnicity. The NLRB changed the environment significantly throughout 1937 as the I.L.W.U aggressively organized interracially and offered a class analysis to contradict the use of racial propaganda (i.e., Japanese workers were loyal to Japan) and other divide and conquer tactics such as favoritism based on race. The ILWU organized and armed workers with the "divide and conquer" *cognitive schema* to recognize such tactics as such. Perhaps most importantly, by connecting the isolated plantation workers to a larger progressive, militant working class movement the organizers offered *a superordinate identity that did not deny race or ethnicity but subsumed it under a larger identity and common purpose.*

The 1937 struggles set the stage for the formation of the interracial movement that would transform Hawai'i. This development was suppressed by martial law imposed on Hawai'i during WWII. Martial law froze wages, made work mandatory, "loaned" workers to the military and mandated severe conditions of work. The overall effect of martial law was to stifle unions and labor organizing and to Hawai'i foment discontent among workers making them more susceptible to the analysis and organizing efforts of the ILWU. After martial law was lifted worker discontent boiled over (Jung, 2006). The ILWU was successful in constructing an ideology (worldview) that would unite the workers interracially *against* employers and ultimately the Big Five by offering an interpretive schema that created a common interracial identity without denying ethnic identity or racial histories. The ILWU practiced inter-racialism by promoting a diverse leadership, holding meetings in multiple languages, insisting on equal opportunity with present employees and thereby creating *equal status contact in the situation.* In 1946 the interracial labor movement struck the sugar industry and won. They had a *successful outcome.* This movement was re-affirmed by successful outcomes in 1947, 1948, 1949 and 1951. There was, then, a succession of positive and successful outcomes from this intergroup cooperation based on equal status in service of a superordinate goal. A *local culture* was nourished by this historical process.

8.7 The Construction of a Superordinate Identity: The Development of Local Culture and Identity

The use of the term "local" has been traced to the infamous Massie Case (1931) to collectively categorize people from Hawai'i in contrast to the White military accusers of Hawaiian and mixed race working class youths accused of kidnapping and raping Thalia Massie. The criteria for being "local" seems to be cultural rather than racial involving adherence to certain values (e.g., *aloha*) including a respect and appreciation of cultural diversity. It represents an appreciation of and commitment to the land, cultures, and peoples of Hawai'i. "Local" identity has been maintained as an expression of resistance and opposition to outside domination. The plantation experience and labor movement undoubtedly facilitated the development of "local" identity where different ethnocultural groups developed a common language that enabled people from many places (e.g., U.S., Japan, Philippines, Samoa, Korea) to communicate with each other. This was passed on to subsequent generations to become a unique language that is, today, English-based, but consists of seven diverse languages employed in the construction of a unique, common system of communication known as pidgin and Hawaiian Creole.

"Local" culture, then, may represent the development of a superordinate identity that may be seen as supplementing but not supplanting original ethnicities. For example, the affirmation of a local identity for the entire Japanese American community is apparent in a statement prominently displayed on a wall in the Historical Gallery of the Japanese Cultural Center of Hawai'i which states "We are no longer only Japanese American, we are local. We have learned from others. We have absorbed their values and traditions while we have preserved our own. We are proud of our mixed heritage-our local Hawaiian way of life (Okumura, 2008, p. 134)." The appreciation of and familiarity with the different peoples and cultures of Hawai'i is, then a major dimension of "local" identity. Embedded in this narrative are the conditions identified by Allport and Pettigrew.

References

Allport, G. W. (1954). *The nature of prejudice*. Reading, MA: Addison-Wesley.

Becker, E. (1971). *The birth and death of meaning* (2nd ed.). New York: Free Press.

Becker, E. (1973). *The denial of death*. New York: Free Press.

Becker, E. (1975). *Escape from evil*. New York: Free Press.

Cialdini, R. B., Wosinska, W., Barrett, D. W., Butner, J., & Gornik-Durose, M. (1999). Compliance with a request in two cultures: The differential influence of social proof and commitment/consistency on collectivists and individualists. *Personality and Social Psychology Bulletin, 25*(10), 1242–1253.

Cooper, G., & Daws, G. (1985). *Land and power in Hawai'i*. Honolulu: University of Hawai'i Press.

Cushner, K., & Brislin, R. W. (1996). *Intercultural interactions: A practical guide* (Vol. 9). Thousand Oaks, CA: Sage Publications.

Erikson, E.H. (1959). *Identity and the life cycle* (Psychological Issues Monograph No.1). New York: International Universities Press.

Fanon, F. (1968). *The wretched of the earth, with a preface by Jean-Paul Sartre, trans. Constance Farrington*. New York: Grove Weidenfeld, 1991.

Goldhagen, D. J. (1996). *Hitler's willing executioners*. New York: Alfred Angelo.

Greenberg, J., Solomon, S., & Pyszczynski, T. (1997). Terror management theory of self-esteem and cultural worldviews: Empirical assessments and conceptual refinements. *Advances in Experimental Social Psychology, 29*, 61–139.

Hassan, F. (2004). Cultural diversity and the prospect of peacebuilding through sharing a we-world. In B. N. Setiadi, A. Supratiknya, W. J. Lonner, & Y. H. Poortinga (Eds.), *Ongoing themes in Psychology and Culture. Selected Papers from the Sixteenth International Association for Cross-Cultural Psychology*. International Association for Cross-Cultural Psychology.

Huntington, S. P. (1996). *The clash of civilizations: Remaking of a world order*. New York: Touchstone.

Jung, M.-K. (2006). *Reworking Race: The making of Hawaii's interracial labor movement*. New York: Columbia University Press.

Laenui, P. (2000). Processes of decolonization. In M. Battiste (Ed.), *Reclaiming indigenous voice and vision* (pp. 150–160). Vancouver, BC: University of British Columbia Press.

Marsella, A. J. (2005). Culture and conflict: Understanding, negotiating, and reconciling conflicting constructions of reality. *International Journal of Intercultural Relations, 29*(6), 651–673.

Maslow, A. H. (1987). *Motivations and Personality, 3. tr.*

McGregor, H. A., Lieberman, J. D., Greenberg, J., Solomon, S., Arndt, J., Simon, L., & Pyszczynski, T. (1998). Terror management and aggression: Evidence that mortality salience motivates aggression against worldview-threatening others. *Journal of Personality and Social Psychology, 74*, 590–605.

Memmi, A. (1965). *The colonizer and the colonized*. Boston, MA: Beacon Press.

Okumura, J. Y. (2008). *Ethnicity and inequality in Hawai'i*. Philadelphia, PA: Temple University Press.

Pettigrew, T. F. (1998). Intergroup contact theory. *Annual Review of Psychology, 49*, 65–85.

Pyszczynski, T., Greenberg, J., & Solomon, S. (1997). Why do we need what we need? A terror management perspective on the roots of human social motivation. *Psychological Inquiry, 8*, 1–20.

Salzman, M. (2001a). Cultural trauma and recovery: Perspectives from terror management theory. *Trauma, Violence & Abuse, 2*(2), 172–191.

Salzman, M. (2001b). Globalization, culture & anxiety. *Journal of Social Distress and the Homeless, 10*(4), 337–352.

Salzman, M. (2003). Existential anxiety, religious fundamentalism, the "clash of civilizations" and terror management theory. *Cross Cultural Psychology Bulletin, 37*(3), 10–16.

Salzman, M. (2012). Ethno-cultural conflict and cooperation in Hawai'i. In D. Landis & R. Albert (Eds.), *Handbook of Ethno-political conflict* (pp. 21–44). New York: Springer.

Sherif, M. (1966). *In common predicament: Social psychology of intergroup conflict and cooperation*. Boston, MA: Houghton Mifflin Company.

Sherif, M., Harvey, O. J., White, B. J., Hood, W. R., & Sherif, C. W. (1954/1961). *Social judgment*. New Haven, CT: Yale University Press

Snyder, M., & Miene, P. (1994). On the functions of stereotypes and prejudice. In *The psychology of prejudice: The Ontario symposium* (Vol. 7, pp. 33–54). Hillsdale, NJ: Lawrence Erlbaum.

Stephan, W. G., & Stephan, C. W. (2000). An integrated threat theory of prejudice. In S. Oskamp (Ed.), *"The Claremont Symposium on Applied Social Psychology" Reducing prejudice and discrimination* (pp. 23–45). Mahwah, NJ: Lawrence Erlbaum Associates.

Chapter 9
Inter-cultural Training

The economy and harmony of every nation depends on how effectively and respectfully internationally and culturally diverse peoples within national boundaries interact with each other. Misunderstandings that might produce conflict, ill feelings and anxiety may occur in cross-cultural interactions with no bad intention. The potential for such outcomes is embedded in the nature of culture and intercultural interactions.

The causes of ethno-cultural conflict are multiple. Considering the vital psychological functions of culture (Salzman, 2001a, 2001b) we are challenged to study and consider how culturally diverse peoples can co-exist in mutually enriching ways rather than descending into misunderstanding and even bloody conflict based on such factors as misattribution of intentions, alternative constructions of reality, competition for material or psychological resources, and efforts to manage anxiety through in-group identification and out-group demonization.

Culture is a critical determinant and mediator of conflict in disputes between individuals, communities, and nations. Culture can be considered both a source of conflict and an essential means of its resolution (Salzman, 2012).

Additionally, it becomes imperative that we grasp the sources of confounding perceptual error that may produce conflict or impede the development of positive intercultural interactions and cross cultural relationships. The consequences of such error may range from misunderstanding and failure to accomplish shared goals to murderous violence. While the negative potentials for inter-cultural interactions exist such contact and engagement may also produce opportunities for mutual enrichment, shared knowledge and a range of solutions to the problems and promises of being human.

In order to address the challenges and positive possibilities inherent in intercultural interactions a variety of training methods have been developed. This chapter will briefly survey the field of intercultural sensitivity training programs and will focus on intercultural simulations as a method used to replicate real intercultural interactions in a game-like context to provide an experiential understanding of the nature of culture and the sources of error embedded in the dynamics of intercultural

M.B. Salzman, *A Psychology of Culture*, International and Cultural Psychology,
https://doi.org/10.1007/978-3-319-69420-7_9

interactions. The simulation known as Bafa-Bafa has been used by the author of this chapter in a variety of culture based university courses (i.e., *Cross-Cultural Counseling, Clinical Work with Diverse Populations, A Psychology of Culture*) and his experience with it shall inform this chapter. Bafa-Bafa was probably the first intercultural simulation developed and was made available in 1974. Subsequently there have been other simulations have been developed but all owe some credit for inspiration to Bafa-Bafa. It is the classic (Pusch, 2004) that has provided a model for those that followed and shall be a primary focus into this inquiry of intercultural simulations and their utility in addressing essential themes, sources of error, learning opportunities and the potentials for confusion, conflict and enrichment inherent in the nature of intercultural interactions.

9.1 Intercultural Simulations in the Broader Context of Intercultural Training

Fowler and Blohm (2004) described and analyzed varying methods used in intercultural training. They described intercultural training methods and categorized them as primarily cognitive, active, or intercultural methods categories. The methods are listed below under the categorization suggested by Fowler and Blohm. A complete description of each method is beyond the scope of this chapter and the reader is referred to their elaboration (Fowler & Bloom, 2004) of these methods, their desired outcomes, adaptability and utility:

Cognitive Methods (focus on knowledge acquisition)

- Lectures
- Written materials
- Computer-based training
- Films, DVDs, Videos
- Self Assessment
- Case Studies
- Critical Incidents

Active Methods (focus on actively involving trainees in some tasks)

- Role Playing
- Simulation Games (i.e., Bafa-Bafa)
- Intercultural exercises (trainees are involved a task related to session content)

Intercultural Methods (designed for intercultural learning, self awareness, competence)

- Contrast Culture (research based)
- Culture Assimilator or Intercultural Sensitizer (attribution training-most research based method)
- Cross-Cultural Analysis

- Cross-Cultural Dialogues
- Area Studies
- Immersion

These methods may be used in combination(s) to effect desired outcomes. It is, of course, imperative to be clear on what outcomes are hoped to be achieved through the training experience. These outcomes included the acquisition of new knowledge, new skills or changed attitudes (i.e., from ethnocentric to ethno-relative or culturally relative). The desired outcomes might be proximal or distal. A proximal outcome such as skill development may seem desirable but the skills may be used in service of a negative distal outcome such as economic exploitation.

Bhawuk (1990) suggested that the ultimate goal of cross-cultural orientations and intercultural training is to make the interaction a "success." Importantly, he notes that for any interaction to be considered successful both parties "must think and feel positively about the interaction (p. 327)." Indeed the term "successful" bears some examination as "success" for one party may lead to the exploitation or effective domination of the other. The inter-culturally knowledgeable and sophisticated missionary or insidious colonial/settler may use cultural knowledge of the "other" in ways that may be disadvantageous or harmful to the missionized, colonized or exploited. As with all knowledge, inter-cultural knowledge maybe used for various purposes. The power dynamics existing between the members of the two interacting cultures and the intent of both parties cannot be ignored, as the purpose of the training must benefit both parties. It is the author's contention that intercultural interactions need to be based on mutual respect and the equalization of status in the situation (Allport, 1954; Pettigrew, 1998) in order to produce "success" where each party benefits.

Numerous other typologies have been proposed to classify existing intercultural training and orientation programs. Bhawuk (1990) summarized various typologies that situate various intercultural training programs along specific dimensions. Triandis (1977), for example has suggested a classification system based on whether the program's focus is *culture-specific* or *culture general* and whether it is primarily cognitively, affectively or behaviorally oriented. Culture specific programs attempt to prepare the learner for successful interactions with people from the target culture while culture-general programs are intended to provide the behavioral and cognitive tools needed to interact successfully with members of different cultural orientation or cultures "in general" that differ from one's own. Gudykunst and Hammer (1983) developed a typology that distinguished between methods that were primarily didactic or experiential and whether the content of the training is culture general or culture specific. Developed a typology on the basis of low, moderate, or high trainee involvement and whether the focus of the training was primarily cognitive, affective or behavioral leading to nine cells where different training methods may be placed and conceptualized. Bhawuk (1990) proposed a classification system differentiated on three axes: trainee involvement varying from low to high, trainer involvement varying from low to high, and the content of the orientation varying from a narrow (culture specific) to a broad (culture general) focus. In his system, Bhawuk locates intercultural simulations in both culturally specific and culture general and high trainer and trainee involvement types of methods. In this system the classic Bafa-Bafa simulation is located in the culture general content sector as well as having high trainer and trainee involvement. Although simulations are experiential in nature a skillful facilitator can lead participants new knowledge, insight, an increase in one's behavioral repertoire and the ability to recognize, identify and overcome such sources of error as the *fundamental attribution error* (Ross, 1977), *ethno-centric and self-serving bias, attributional bias* (Salzman, 1995), *the homogeneity bias* (Linville, 1998) *and the nature of in-group/ out-group dynamics* (Tajfel, 1979).

The "cultural assimilator" or "intercultural sensitizer" is an example of a cognitively oriented approach that seeks to allow access to the attributional tendencies and perspectives of the target culture that the learner hopes to understand better in order to interact positively with members of the target culture. Albert (1983) summarized a substantial body of research and found evidence that an ICS (culture specific) is an effective in imparting cultural information, for increasing the isomorphic attributions (i.e., convergent with the host culture) of the learners and for facilitating interpersonal relations between trainees and members of the target culture. She also found that the ICS could positively affect task performance.

The construction of these instruments is labor intensive and systematic. The first step (Albert, 1983) is to identify critical incidents where the culturally different interactants experience bad feelings or misunderstandings that may lead to conflict when there is in fact no bad intentions just differential attributions of the meanings of the behaviors or situations. Numerous intercultural sensitizers (ICS) or "assimilators" have been developed and at least one "culture general" assimilator based on the identification of 18 themes common to intercultural interactions (Cushner & Brislin, 1996). In the case of the culture general assimilator the critical incidents are constructed from the 18 themes identified by Cushner and Brislin. These two types of ICS's, culture-specific and culture general could be classified as a cognitively based approach seeking to equip the learner with the ability to make isomorphic attributions or attributions of meaning consistent with how target culture members tend to interpret behaviors, situations and interactions. The ICS, as with a skillfully processed simulation, might provide a means to overcome several sources of error such as the *fundamental attribution error* identified by Ross (1977) where the observer tends to attribute cause to the actor while missing the context of the action which may make the action more accurately interpretable and culture is context. History is context. Narratives and stories transmitted across generations are context. Worldviews and descriptions of reality are context. A well-constructed ICS (Albert, 1983) has the ability to make context salient to the observer. The stages of the development of an ICS as outlined by Albert are as follows:

- Generation of Episodes: this is the critical incident (CI) technique developed by Flanagan (1954). A CI is an incident that produces misunderstanding, problems, confusion or conflict between people from two different cultures. A CI is sufficiently complete to permit inferences about the meaning of the behaviors or situations.

- Episode Selection and Construction: In order to select productive and appropriate CI's a bi-cultural panel is organized to review the raw incidents and provide a cultural or historical context for the observed behavior or situations. This is a critical stage. In the cases of "A Navajo Intercultural Sensitizer" the panel was given veto power over what they wished to share of their culture given the unfortunate history of western research "on" (not with) indigenous peoples (Smith, 2012).
- Attribution Elicitation: The task here is to identify the attributions given by the two cultural samples. Questions to elicit the attributions focus on the thoughts, feelings and behaviors of the participants in the incident.
- Attribution Selection: The elicited attributions are then empirically tested to determine if the elicited attributions differentiate the cultural groups, and which attributions each group more frequently preferred. Those incidents that differentiated the groups are included in the ICS.

The final ICS consists of an episode (CI) followed by a question concerning the likely thoughts, feelings, or behaviors of the participants. The question is followed by four alternative attributions where one of the attributions represent the most frequently chosen by the host culture members and the trainee's culture members. Following each response choice relevant (provided by panel) cultural and historical context that illuminates the meaning of the behavior.

The author has constructed a Navajo Intercultural Sensitizer (Salzman, 1990) focusing on problematic interactions between Navajo and Non-Navajo school personnel and Navajo students and advised on the construction of a Hawaiian ICS targeting interactions between Native Hawaiian students and non-Hawaiian professors therefore this method is further explored and its effects examined. For, example, "A Navajo Intercultural Sensitizer" (Salzman, 1990) allows the learner access to essential historical contexts such as the experience of dehumanizing racism that are not universally shared but historical context made salient provides an interpretive lens through which the meaning behaviors may be attributed more accurately. The cultural and historical feedback offered by the bilingual and bicultural panel can provide the necessary context through which isomorphic attributions can be accomplished thereby reducing the confounding effects of the *fundamental attribution error*. The well-constructed ICS may illuminate, for example, the meaning and function of "small talk" in the two cultures by making the cultural context of the behavior salient and the relevant and the meaning of the behavior more accurately interpretable. In the Navajo ICS incidents revealed the meaning of gestures (i.e., pointing with lips not fingers because pointing with finger might indicate an accusation of witchcraft); restrictions on the use of "touch"; taboos (i.e., talking or joking about death); spiritual beliefs; the sacred meaning of "the land"; the respect shown to the thoughts of children; and meaning of silence and pause. In order to avoid stereotyping with-in group variation was reported in percentages as well as statistical procedures to test group differences.

9.2 Intercultural Simulations

Simulations are training activities that may include game-like elements such as goals, payoffs, and constraints (Fowler & Blohm, 2004). They may be organized around known dimensions that tend to vary across cultures (Hofstede, 2001; Hofstede & Pedersen, 2002; Hofstede, 2002). Intercultural simulations have created two cultures that differ on these dimensions and task the participants with interacting with each other in order to simulate real cultural differences and how they might influence the interactions and the results of the interactions. Hofstede (2002), in his seminal work on national comparisons of values, behaviors, institutions and organizations identified the following cultural (national level) dimensions. A brief description of each is offered (Brislin, 1993):

Individualism-Collectivism: In individualistic cultures personal goals and identity are emphasized and consideration of individual goals takes precedence over group goals. The United States is considered to be a highly individualistic national culture. In collectivist cultures identity and goals is related to group membership. A Native American colleague once stated to the author "I am my relations." When interacting in collectivist cultures people are not seen as just individuals but also as members of some group.

Power-Distance: Refers to cultures based on more or less equality. It is the relative amount of power high status groups have relative to low status groups. In low power distance cultures people feel free to disagree and laws and norms that make power differences as minimal as possible guide behavior. The U.S. is considered to be a low power distance national culture.

Masculinity-Femininity: In general values such as aggressiveness, assertiveness, and competitiveness are considered "masculine" and concern with relationships, cooperation, and tenderness and taking other people's feelings into account are considered "feminine" values. In "feminine" national cultures there is more of a tendency for genders to share power and for women to develop an effective political voice. Gender roles are less rigid. Scandinavian national cultures tend to be more "feminine" and Japan is highly masculine as men hold power.

Uncertainty-Avoidance: Although all cultures are concerned with uncertainty national cultures that are high in "uncertainty avoidance" (UA) have large numbers of rules and people are socialized to believe that uncertainty about the future is best dealt with if everyone behaves according to widely accepted guidelines and norms. High UA national cultures have many rules and norms to reduce uncertainty

The classic simulation Bafa-Bafa can be seen to reflect and embed a number of these dimensions in the exercise (i.e., individualism-collectivism, power distance, masculinity-femininity). Although simulations are experiential in nature a skillful facilitator can lead participants new knowledge, insight, an increase in one's behavioral repertoire and the ability to recognize, identify and overcome such sources of error as the *fundamental attribution error* (Ross, 1977), *ethno-centric and self-serving bias, attributional bias* (Salzman, 1995), *the homogeneity bias* (Linville, 1998) *and the nature of in-group/out-group dynamics* (Tajfel, 1979).

Intercultural simulations may reveal important potentially confounding aspects of actual intercultural interactions. Sources of perceptual error and their behavioral consequences may be abstracted from the experiential nature of simulations. One predictable source of error is the *fundamental attribution error* (FAE). It is thought by some (Ross, 1977) to form the conceptual bedrock for the field of social psychology. The FAE describes the cognitive tendency to predominantly over-value dispositional (factors within the actor) personality-based explanations for the observed behaviors of others, thereby under-valuing or failing to acknowledge the potential power of situational attributions or situational explanations for the behavioral motives of others. In other words the power of the situation is overlooked and cause is presumed to be located within the actor we observe. The situation is context. History is context. Culture is context. Intercultural training may be effective to the degree that context is made salient and that predictable errors and attributional biases are addressed and overcome. The fundamental attribution error has been identified (Salzman, 1995) as the tendency to attribute cause to dispositional factors within the actor while contextual factors such as history and culture are not considered or fade into the distant background. One explanation for this tendency is that actors and observers differ in their points of view. The situation (i.e., culture, history) is salient to the actor but the actor is salient to the observer leading to a tendency to attribute different meanings to the behavior. A number of "de-biasing" techniques have been found effective in reducing the effect of the FAE. These include noting consensus information. If most people in a group behave in the same way when put in the same situation then the situation is more likely to be the primary cause of the behavior. Therefore attributing cause to the actor may contribute to perceptual and attributional error. In addition one is would be well advised to look for unseen causes and less immediately salient factors such as culture. A skilled facilitator, conducting an intercultural simulation, can bring this and other sources of error to saliency and insight.

Other sources of error may develop out of a need to satisfy and defend the self-esteem motive. The *ethno-centric and self-serving biases* derive from the need to protect or enhance one's private image. In the case of the *self-serving* bias there is a tendency to attribute more responsibility to the self for favorable outcomes than for unfavorable outcomes (Greenberg, Pyszczynski, & Solomon, 1982) consequently when an intercultural interaction fails and produces negative affect the "other" is held responsible. When the interaction succeeds the opposite attribution tends to occur. In the case of the *ethno-centric* bias several studies (e.g., Greenberg & Rosenfield, 1979) have shown that there is a bias in the attributions used to explain the behavior of in-group and out-group members. That is, when an in-group member does something well it is explained in terms of some underlying trait such as intelligence while if an out-group member does something equally well the performance tends to be attributed to such situational factors as luck. The opposite tends to be true of negative behaviors or performance as the out-group member's behavior is explained in terms of stable and enduring traits (i.e., "that's just how they are").

The homogeneity bias (Linville, 1998) refers to the tendency of people to perceive less variability among their out-groups than among their comparable in-groups.

This out-group homogeneity effect provides a sense of predictability but is a source of error through stereotypical overgeneralization that may preclude accurate judgments. The relative difference between perceived heterogeneity of in-groups and out-groups has been referred to as the "out-group homogeneity effect." This tendency nourishes the perception that "we are diverse but you are all alike" or "they all look alike."

Tajfel, 1979, has illuminated the power of *in-group/out-group dynamics* that associated with the need for self-identity and differentiation from others. The Mininimal Group Paradigm is a term used in social psychology experiments (e.g. Tajfel, 1970; Sherif, Harvey, White, Hood, & Sherif, 1954) where people are randomly assigned to groups. These studies have shown that simply being randomly assigned to be a member of a group is enough to change behavior. The Robber's Cave experiment (Sherif et al., 1954) is one of social psychology's most cited studies dealing with differentiation, showing how easily opposing in-groups and group hostilities can form. A phenomenon occurs where group members will begin to associate superiority to their group over and above other out-groups. In-group members associate their self-esteem through positive social comparisons with other groups where their group is seen as superior. The insights offered by Social Identity Theory (Tajfel, 1970) concerning the people's tendencies to derive and enhance self-esteem by identifying with specific social groups and to divide the social world into "us" and "them" suggest a powerful psychological motivation that must be acknowledged and addressed if positive intercultural relations are to be developed. For the barriers to positive intercultural relations represented by these sources or error to be overcome it is necessary to acknowledge, understand and address them. It is necessary to consider their contributions to our judgments about ourselves and "others" as the consequences of error may range from the trivial to the destructive. Intercultural training needs to account for these factors

These sources of error may be brought to salience through intercultural simulations by a skillful facilitation of the debriefings and discussion following the experiential exercise.

9.3 Strengths and Weaknesses of Intercultural Simulations

Fowler and Bloom (2004) identified strengths and challenges of the simulation method of intercultural training. They note that simulations may take time (3 or more hours) and preparation of materials. Most importantly, the debriefing, which is key to the success of the exercise, requires a skillful facilitation to bring out the essential lessons of the experience. Strengths include the opportunity to practice new skills, reflect on their experience, process their emotions and achieve insight. In addition to the sources of perceptual and attributional error previously mentioned themes may be identified that are common in intercultural interactions. Cushner and Brislin (1996) identified 18 such themes. The author requires students to address which of these themes they experienced in the simulation. They include:

- Anxiety: How we respond to the state of anxiety is consequential. Social psychology has provided evidence (Greenberg, Solomon, & Pyszczynski, 1997; Salzman, 2001a, 2001b) that culture may serve as an anxiety buffer against the terror inherent in human existence by making anxiety-buffering self-esteem available to its adherents and "believers". Consequently, especially under certain conditions (i.e., mortality salience), cultural differences maybe inherently threatening because they call into question the absolute "truth" of one's worldview and belief system.
- Disconfirmed expectations: People from the "other" culture may respond to one's behavior in unpredictable ways. Our expectations are, to a great extent, culturally mediated.
- Belonging: To feel included and a sense of belonging is a human need and rejection due to culturally inappropriate behavior that is misunderstood may be extremely aversive. In the course of the Bafa-Bafa it is likely that someone will experience exclusion and rejection due to well-meaning behaviors that violate cultural norms and protocols. The processing of this experience needs to be handled with care and sensitivity in order to reduce defensiveness and maximize insight.
- Ambiguity: The messages one receives may not be accurately interpreted and guidance for acceptable behaviors may not be clear. One cannot be sure what responses our behaviors might elicit.
- Confrontations with one's prejudices: When one applies values and appraisals from one's own culture to intercultural interactions negative judgments about the "other" are likely.
- In-group/Outgroup distinction: People entering another culture need to be sensitive to the fact that they will often be out-group members and subject to the in-group/out-group dynamics described earlier. Social identity theory (Tajfel, 1970) and exercises using a minimal group paradigm, as in randomly assigning students into an "Alpha" or "Beta" culture in the Bafa-Bafa exercise, indicate how our self-esteem is connected to the social groups we identify with.
- Attribution: The meanings attributed to behaviors and situations may differ across cultures. The ICS is specifically designed to allow access to the attributions members of the "other" culture tend to make. A skillful facilitator of intercultural simulations can also reveal the attributional tendencies that may produce bad feelings, misunderstandings or conflict.

Fowler and Bloom (2004) suggest that one of the real strengths of simulations is their versatility. They can reveal value differences, sources or perceptual and attributional error, communication barriers, the logic of the rules and norms of the "other" culture in the context of history and ecology, the error inherent in applying judgments based on one's own cultural framework to a people who may in fact live in a totally different social reality. The author had this experience when he journeyed from his community to an impoverished racially tense inner city community in Brooklyn. It became clear to the young teacher (the author) that his students and their families lived in a social reality that the young teacher was quite clueless about.

9.4 Examples of Existing Intercultural Simulations

A list of intercultural simulations is available (http://www.carla.umn.edu/culture/resources/exercises.html) on line and a brief review of some examples of these follows:

Aid to Minorians/*Intercultural Source Book* (1995):

Participants are divided into two groups: the Minorians are a poor and underdeveloped society; while the Majorians are wealthy and are trying to plan a project to help the Minorians. Cultural assumptions and the relationship between donor and receiving parties are examined. Issues of class and privilege become salient.

The Albatross (Gochenour, 1977):

This is a nonverbal role-playing exercise that may include a variety of themes such as male-female relationships and the issue of privilege. Participants are asked to watch a brief role-play and then describe what they saw. Most will interpret what they saw and judge what they saw having not heard anything in this non-verbal role-play. This simulation offers the opportunity to appreciate how we give meaning to events based on our own experience as we superimpose our experience to new observations. This may be a source of error.

Barnga (Steinwachs 1995; Thiagarajan 1990):

A nonverbal game in which participants are divided into groups to learn a card game based on a number of simple rules. The participants do not know that each group's set of rules is slightly different, so when they begin to play the game with the others conflict develops. Of course, in reality cultures have differing rules and norms and this is reflected in the Barnga simulation. This simulation demonstrates how quickly ingroup-outgroup dynamics form.

Ecotonos (Saphiere 1995):

Participants take on roles as members of different cultural groups and are then asked to interact with the others to solve a problem. This simulation looks at how homogenous and heterogeneous groups work and the assumptions made about decision-making processes and how to address a problem. This may reveal how our unspoken assumptions guide problem-solving behaviors.

Grocery Store (Eun & Patton, 1996):

This exercise simulates a diverse neighborhood in the inner city where tensions arise between diverse culture groups. A critical incident occurs and is interpreted differently by each party. This simulation focuses on race relations, cultural diversity and the different cultural meanings attributed to different behaviors. A good debriefing of this exercise might reveal the relevant cultural and historical contexts that inform these attributions.

IDE-GO (Fowler & Mumford, 1995):

Participants separate into two groups; one simulates North American culture while the other simulates South American culture. The game is designed to provide insight into the interaction processes and behaviors of these two groups. This is a culture-specific approach.

Star Power (Shirts, 2013) Simulation Training Systems:

Participants form groups with different economic statuses and seek to trade with each other to improve their economic statuses. The most economically viable group is allowed to alter the rules. Alliances develop and ingroup-outgroup dynamics are manifested and assumptions about the uses and abuses of power may be revealed.

The Owl (Gochenour, 1977):

This simulation involves a group of reporters on assignment to interview members of another country and, if they act appropriately, they will gain access to a mysterious cultural event. If they are successful they have their story. However communication problems arise and the "reporters" face the dilemma of needing information while searching for culturally appropriate ways to ask for it.

As previously stated in the introduction Bafa-Bafa was probably the first intercultural simulation developed and was made available in 1974. Subsequently there have been other simulations have been developed but all owe some credit for inspiration to Bafa-Bafa. It is the classic (Pusch, 2004) that has provided a model for those that followed and shall be a primary focus into this inquiry of intercultural simulations and their utility in addressing essential themes, sources of error, learning opportunities and the potentials for confusion, conflict and enrichment inherent in the nature of intercultural interactions.

9.5 BAFA-BAFA: A Specific Example

The classic simulation Bafa-Bafa can, with skillful facilitation, reveal a number of Hofstede's (2002) dimensions of cultural variability (i.e., individualism-collectivism, power distance, masculinity-femininity) as well as typical sources of error that may confound positive intercultural interactions, create prejudice a promote ineffective behaviors. Although simulations are experiential in nature a skillful facilitator can lead participants new knowledge, insight, an increase in one's behavioral repertoire, and the ability to recognize, identify and overcome such sources of perceptual and attributional error as the *fundamental attribution error* (Ross, 1977), *ethno-centric and self-serving bias* (Greenberg et al., 1982), *attributional bias* (Salzman, 1995), *the homogeneity bias* (Linville, 1998) *and the nature of in-group/out-group dynamics* (Tajfel, 1979). A skillful facilitator may, in the debriefing following the experience of the simulation, help participants see how inter-cultural interactions may be affected by cultural variation in norms, values, and sources of self-esteem. In addition, it is both possible and advisable to identify essential psychological functions of culture such as the prescriptive pathways to self-esteem construction through a belief in the cultural worldview and seeing oneself as meeting the standards of value prescribed by the culture. This aspect of culture suggests that while self-esteem (defined as seeing oneself as having value in a meaningful world) is a universal psychological need it is constructed differently across cultures. Each of these will be examined. Self-esteem, often trivialized, is a vital psychological resource that represents powerful human motivation. Indeed, Becker (1971) called it the dominant human motivation. Alfred Adler is quoted as follows "The supreme law of (life) is this: the sense of worth of the self shall not be allowed to be diminished" (in Ansbacher & Ansbacher, 1946, p. 358). In Bafa-Bafa the sources of self-esteem are different and motivating.

The author has had extensive experience with this simulation and has utilized in a variety of courses where culture is a focal concern. In courses such as *Clinical Work with Diverse Populations, Cross-Cultural Counseling,* and *A Psychology of Culture* the author has used this simulations early in the semester to bring to salience the impact of culture on individuals, groups and inter-cultural interactions over a period of 23 years. Following a brief description of the exercise and I will describe what aspects of intercultural relations are possible to identify and experience in the Bafa-Bafa simulation. Students, at the outset of the simulation are instructed to pay close attention to their feelings, thoughts and behaviors in the course of the exercise. In addition to common sources of perceptual and attributional error and Hofstede's dimensions of cultural variability students are provided with the 18 themes in inter-cultural interactions identified by Cushner and Brislin (1996) and are directed to indicate which of these were observed or experienced. The students are given the assignment to write a reaction/reflection paper describing their experience in the light of the issues presented above.

The Bafa-Bafa simulation begins with the construction of two cultures that differ on number attributes of cultural variation including norms, values, behavioral expectations, protocols, customs and sources of self-esteem. The cultures are named Alpha and Beta. Students are randomly assigned to either Alpha or Beta cultures and acculturated into the values, rules and expectations of their assigned culture. This process surprisingly takes only about 20 min. Once participants seem comfortable with their "new culture" observers are exchanged for a brief visit where they observe "their" ways and behaviors. The observers are charged with conducting a non-verbal observation to assess and hypothesized how "they" are and how best to interact with "them" "successfully." The observers then report back to their home cultures and share their hypotheses with them. At this point visitors are exchanged, given the artifacts needed in the visited culture and instructed to observe and then attempt interactions based on their and the observers observations. When all of the visits are completed a break is given and the groups are given a break with the instruction or returning to the main room but sitting together with their home cultures on opposite sides of the room. A debriefing then is conducted to bring out the insights possible from the simulation. They are assigned the reaction/reflection paper.

Alpha and Beta cultures are quite different in ways replicating real cultural differences that exist in the world. Alphans are relaxed and value intimacy in their relations with fellow Alphans within a sexist, patriarchal structure. There are rigid protocols for these interactions that are strictly enforced. The quality of the personal interactions in support of cultural values is much more valued than material gain. Betas on the other hand value success in the marketplace and material rewards. They tend to be egalitarian and competitive where status is gained by accumulating the most "points" in their trading system. We can see here how self-esteem is pursued be both Alphas and Betas but constructed differently. This is but one of the important insights that may be gained from this and other simulations.

9.6 "Gems" That May Be Extracted from the Simulation

Bafa-Bafa has embedded within it several of Hofstede's dimensions of cultural variability. The exercise begins with an orientation that describes the procedures of the simulation. Students are randomly assigned to one of the two cultures and are oriented to their new culture. This cultural orientation is given in separate rooms and includes a description of the values expectation and custom of the two cultures. Alpha culture is described as relaxed valuing touch, personal contact and intimacy within a very rigid hierarchical, patriarchical structure. The sexist nature of this culture, as warm it appears, is explicit in the cultural orientation of the Alphas. They are told that "women are considered to be the property of men" and that "the men are honored and women are considered to be the property of men. Accordingly men may approach either sex but women may only approach other women" (Shirts, 1971). There is a rigid protocol to follow upon greeting a fellow Alphan. The "patriarch" formally signs in all Alphans to the new culture. If there are non-Alphans visiting Alpha culture they will not know of this requirement or the protocols of interaction (e.g., standing close, touching, talking about male relative in hierarchical order, then playing a game where winning was not an objective but the joyous quality of the interaction was the culture affirming goal). Alphans are instructed that any male not approved of by the patriarch who approaches an Alpha female the values of Alpha culture and the "manhood of each male is threatened." Such a violation requires that the offender be isolated and expelled from the Alpha world. It is almost inevitable that an unsuspecting Beta visitor will make this error and be expelled. In Hofstedian terms the Alphas may be considered to be a vertically collectivist culture where the group is most important and upholding the cultural drama (Becker, 1971) and its protocols is of paramount importance. "Winning" the game is not important it is the quality of the relationship and the interaction that wins approval and acceptance. In Cushner and Brislin's (1996) description of 18 themes common in intercultural interactions they note that the desire and need to feel a sense of belonging is often difficult due to the status of outsider who violates cultural norms. When an unsuspecting Beta is expelled from Alpha land for approaching an Alphan female his emotions become engaged which may inflame negative cognitions and even behavior. This scenario requires the facilitator to monitor this interaction and provide appropriate explanations in the debriefing.

Beta culture provides a different pathway to self-esteem. They trade with each other to accumulate points and resultant status. There are few rules as they compete for the points that motivate them. It is a competitive rather egalitarian culture that is only interested in accumulations and not human relationship. In Hofstedian terms the Betas might be considered Individualistic. The two cultures also differ along the Power-Distance continuum. Alphas, being sexist and patriarchical, would rate as high Power Distance while the relatively equal status Betas might be described as a low Power-Distance culture. The Betas also have their own language that will seem strange to the visitors as they try to interact "successfully" with Betas. A skillful facilitator strives to extract the "gems" from the experience during the debriefing.

The *fundamental attribution error* may be revealed through the debriefing questions suggested asking members of each culture to describe (i.e., "Alphas are.... Betas are") the "other." This is followed by asking both cultures to explain themselves and their behaviors in terms of their cultural norms and values. By bringing the culture to salience the learners can realize that seems irrational, confusing, contradictory or unimportant may seem rational, consistent, and affirming to persons in the "other" culture. As previously stated, behavior may be incomprehensible or misinterpreted if de-contextualized from the culture it emerges from.

The debriefing begins with each cultural group, sitting together on opposite sides of the common room describing the "other." This provides an opportunity to consider the *ethno-centric and self-serving biases* as the facilitator takes note of the value laden terms the two groups describe each other and can be used to reveal the "gem" that one is likely to seriously misinterpret the behavior of culturally different "others" if one evaluates "them" only in terms of one's own values, expectations and behavior. Importantly, the simulation provides an opportunity to reveal the attributional biases (Salzman, 1995) that may confound inter-cultural interactions because different cultures often interpret the same events differently. The previously described *Intercultural Sensitizer* is designed to overcome attributional errors by making culture salient. By making the culture salient the *fundamental attribution error* may be revealed and an important lesson taught. The *ethno-centric and self-serving biases* may serve self-esteem protective functions and emerge from the in-group/out-group dynamics described earlier. When interactions "fail" or produce bad feelings and misunderstandings the "other" is likely to be held responsible and oneself relatively blameless. One of the debriefing questions suggested is to ask members of each group which group they would prefer to belong to if there was a choice. Most often, in the author's experience, Alphas tend to prefer being Alpha and Betas prefer to be Betas. Surprisingly this is often true of Alpha females even though it is an explicitly sexist, patriarchical culture. This may be a question of in-group loyalty. It has impressed the author how quickly this develops as has been shown in the *minimal group paradigm* (Tajfel, 1971) studies. In the reaction papers such loyalty is often expressed in such terms as "Alphas rule." It seems clear that when groups are formed they exert a powerful influence on behavior, cognitions and affect.

One "gem" that may be extracted from the simulation is the issue of Cultural Relativity and its limits. What is truly universal, and what is culturally specific and adaptive to particular ecological requirements. There is much to be gleaned from this exercise. Cultural practices that may make sense in a particularly ecological context may be horrifying to an observer from outside of that context. This issue produces important and sensitive questions and challenges both the facilitator and participants explore the limits of cultural relativity. Can any practice be justified because it is "cultural" or are there bottom lines that are universal? The Universal Declaration of Human Rights is an attempt to establish such bottom lines, but has been criticized as a Western imposition (Dela Cruz et al., 2006). The question of the limits of cultural relativity is addressed by one of the debriefing questions suggested by Shirts (1973):

If culture "z" met the needs and aspirations of its members better than culture "y" met the needs of its members, would culture "z" be a better culture than culture "y?"

This question might be followed by what may be the most disturbing dilemma for cultural relativists:

Suppose the members of culture "m" believed that it was good to mutilate young female children and their cultural norms and mores made it possible for this "good" to be realized. Would it be a better or worse culture than culture "o" in which all members of the society were encouraged to grow intellectually, socially and physically as much as they could and the cultural norms and mores made it possible for these goals to be realized?

The participants are further challenged by the question:

How should a visitor react the culture "m"? Try to reform it, adapt to it, tolerate it?

The development of multiculturalism marked a well-justified movement and reaction to the imposition of Western "pseudo-etics" on culturally diverse populations. Now we consider the limits of that reaction. Is anything o.k. if it is "cultural?" Are all cultures of equivalent validity and value? These are difficult questions to address as we consider inter-cultural relations, multiculturalism and the possible limits of cultural relativity. These questions can only be adequately addressed while looking deeply into the nature of culture itself, its adaptive function in specific ecological contexts, and its psychological functions for anxiety prone human beings. Inter-cultural simulations such as Bafa-Bafa can be powerful tools in revealing the issues embedded in inter-cultural contact and that may produce misunderstandings, conflict or positive growth and development.

References

Albert, R. A. (1983). The intercultural sensitizer or culture assimilator: A cognitive approach. In D. Landis & R. Brislin (Eds.), *Handbook of intercultural training* (Vol. II, pp. 186–217). New York: Pergamon.

Allport, G. W. (1954). *The nature of prejudice*. Reading, MA: Addison-Wesley.

Ansbacher, H., & Ansbacher, R. (1946). *The individual psychology of Alfred Adler*. New York: Basic Books.

Becker, E. (1971). *The birth and death of meaning: An interdisciplinary perspective on the problem of man* (2nd ed.). New York: Free Press.

Bhawuk, D. P. S. (1990). Cross-cultural orientation programs. In R. Brislin (Ed.), *Applied cross-cultural psychology* (pp. 325–346). Thousand Oaks, CA: Sage.

Brislin, R. W. (1993). *Understanding culture's influence on behavior*. Fort Worth, TX: Harcourt Brace Jovanovich.

Dela Cruz, K., Salzman, M. B., Brislin, R., & Losch, N. (2006). Hawaiian attributional perspectives on intercultural interactions in higher education: Development of an intercultural sensitizer. *International Journal of Intercultural Relations, 30*(1), 119–140.

Cushner, K., & Brislin, R. W. (1996). *Intercultural interactions: A practical guide* (2nd ed.). Thousand Oaks, CA: Sage.

Eun, D., & Patton, B. (1996). The grocery store. In *Program on Negotiation*. Cambridge, MA: Harvard Law School.

Flanagan, J. C. (1954). The critical incident technique. *Psychological Bulletin, 51*, 327–358.

Fowler, S. M., & Mumford, M. G. (1995). *Intercultural sourcebook: Cross-cultural training methods*. Yarmouth, ME: Intercultural Press.

Fowler, S. M., & Blohm, J. M. (2004). An analysis of methods of intercultural training. In D. Landis, J. M. Bennett, & M. J. Bennett (Eds.), *Handbook of intercultural training* (3rd ed., pp. 37–84). Thousand Oaks, CA: Sage.
Gochenour, T. (1977). The owl and the albatross. In D. Batchelder & E. G. Warner (Eds.), *Beyond experience*. Brattleboro VT: Experiment Press.
Greenberg, J., Pyszczynski, T., & Solomon, S. (1982). The self-serving attributional bias: Beyond self-presentation. *Journal of Experimental Social Psychology, 18*(1), 56–67.
Greenberg, J., & Rosenfield, D. (1979). Whites' ethnocentrism and their attributions for the behavior of blacks: A motivational bias. *Journal of Personality, 47*(4), 643–657.
Greenberg, J., Solomon, S., & Pyszczynski, T. (1997). Terror management theory of self-esteem and cultural worldviews: Empirical assessments and conceptual refinements. In M. P. Zanna (Ed.), *Advances in experimental social psychology* (Vol. 29, pp. 61–139). San Diego, CA: Academic.
Gudykunst, W. B., & Hammer, M. R. (1983). Basic training design: Approaches to intercultural training. In D. Landis & R. W. Brislin (Eds.), *Handbook of intercultural training: Issues in theory and design* (Vol. 1, pp. 118–154). Elmsford, NY: Pergamon.
Hofstede, G. (2001). *Culture's consequences: Comparing values, behaviors, institutions and organizations across nations* (2nd ed.). Thousand Oaks, CA: Sage.
Hofstede, G. (2002). Dimensions do not exist: A reply to Brendan McSweeney. *Human Relations, 55*(11), 1355–1361.
Hofstede, G. J., & Pedersen, P. (2002). *Exploring culture: Exercises, stories and synthetic cultures*. London: Nicholas Brealey Publishing.
Linville, P. W. (1998). *The heterogeneity of homogeneity*.
Pettigrew, T. F. (1998). Intergroup contact theory. *Annual Review of Psychology, 49*(1), 65–85.
Pusch, M. D. (2004). Intercultural training in historical perspective. In D. Landis, J. M. Bennett, & M. J. Bennett (Eds.), *Handbook of intercultural training* (3rd ed., pp. 13–36). Thousand Oaks, CA: Sage.
Ross, L. (1977). The intuitive psychologist and his shortcomings: Distortions in the attribution process. *Advances in Experimental Social Psychology, 10*, 173–220.
Salzman, M. (1990). The construction of an intercultural sensitizer for training non-Navajo personnel. *The Journal of American Indian Education, 30*, 25–33.
Salzman, M. (1995). Attributional discrepancies and biases in cross-cultural interactions. *The Journal of Multicultural Counseling and Development, 23*, 181–193.
Salzman, M. B. (2001a). Globalization, culture, and anxiety: Perspectives and predictions from terror management theory. *Journal of Social Distress and the Homeless, 10*(4), 337–352.
Salzman, M. (2001b). Cultural trauma and recovery: Perspectives from terror management theory. *Trauma, Violence & Abuse, 2*(2), 172–191.
Salzman, M. (2012). Dehumanization as a prerequisite of atrocity and killing. In D. J. Christie & J. E. Pim (Eds.), *Nonkilling psychology* (pp. 107–124). Honolulu, HI: Global Center for Non-Killing.
Saphiere, D. M. H. (1995). Ecotonos: A multicultural problem-solving simulation. In S. M. Fowler & M. G. Mumford (Eds.), *Intercultural sourcebook cross-cultural training methods* (Vol. 1, pp. 83–91). Boston: Intercultural Press.
Sherif, M., Harvey, O. J., White, B. J., Hood, W. R., & Sherif, C. W. (1954). *Experimental study of positive and negative intergroup attitudes between experimentally produced groups. Robber's Cave Study*. Norman, OK: University of Oklahoma Press.
Shirts, R. G. (1971). Review of 'Games for Growth' by AK Gordon. *Simulation and Games, 2*(3), 377–379.
Shirts, G. (1973). *BAFA-BAFA: A cross-cultural simulation*. Del Mar, CA: Simile II.
Shirts, G. (2013). *Starpower*. Del Mar, CA: Simile II.
Steinwachs, B. (1995). Barnga: A game for all seasons. In S. M. Fowler & M. G. Mumford (Eds.), *Intercultural Sourcebook, (1): Cross-cultural training methods*. Boston: Intercultural Press.
Tajfel, H. (1970). Experiments in intergroup discrimination. *Scientific American, 223*, 96–102.
Tajfel, H. (1979). Individuals and groups in social psychology. *British Journal of Clinical Psychology, 18*(2), 183–190.
Thiagarajan, S. (1990). *Barnga*. Yarmouth, ME: Intercultural Press.
Triandis, H. (1977). Theoretical framework for evaluation of cross-cultural training effectiveness. *International Journal of Intercultural Relations, 1*, 19–45.

Chapter 10
Conclusions

As stated in the introduction, we are challenged to study and consider how culturally diverse peoples can co-exist in mutually enriching ways rather than descending into misunderstanding and even bloody conflict based on such factors as misattribution of intentions, alternative constructions of reality, competition for material or psychological resources, and efforts to manage anxiety through in-group identification and out-group demonization. It is a serious challenge cultural differences may create and fuel deadly conflict (Marsella, 2005) or even a "clash of civilizations" (Huntington, 1996). Such conflict, as most phenomena have multiple and interactive causes. Some of these have been described in this chapter. The challenge of multiculturalism is to maximize its positive potentials and to recognize the sources and potentials for conflict. Inter-cultural training and the specific methods described in this chapter are an attempt to reveal the nature, promise, and perils of intercultural relations. Becker (1971) described culture as the highest form of human adaptation. It presents solutions to the problems of living as human beings in the varied ecological niches from which they arise. It can be argued that cultural diversity, like bio-diversity, makes survival more probable. Life is hard and humans are challenged to meet its demands. We need access to all the solutions that are available to address the challenges of being human. Cultures may be viewed as offering possible solutions to the existential questions of *how to be* and *how to act* in order to make survival more probable and most importantly *survive as what*? This is the promise of multiculturalism. The perspectives taken in this book are grounded in the human condition itself. They are:

In the beginning there are needs. Human needs.
Humans are motivated to satisfy their needs.
Cultures address human needs.
Humans may seek to satisfy their perceived needs with positive or destructive behaviors.
Needs are both physiological and psychological.
Among these needs is the need for meaning

M.B. Salzman, *A Psychology of Culture*, International and Cultural Psychology,
https://doi.org/10.1007/978-3-319-69420-7_10

Humans are motivated to satisfy the need for meaning.
Self-esteem, a primary psychological resource, can only be constructed in a world of meaning.
Humans have an existential problem. We are mortal and know it.
Humans are anxiety-prone organisms.
Self-esteem is culturally constructed as serves as a defense against the terror inherent in the human condition
Cultures offer a "roadmap" for living and achieving a sense of value.
Cultures may serve as an immortality ideology because by one can then feel part of something larger than self and that continues beyond one's mortal life. Therefore, cultures address core human needs physiological and psychological.

Peace!

References

Becker, E. (1971). *The birth and death of meaning* (2nd ed.). New York: Free Press.
Huntington, S. P. (1996). *The clash of civilizations: Remaking of a world order*. New York: Touchstone.
Marsella, A. J. (2005). Culture and conflict: Understanding, negotiating, and reconciling conflicting constructions of reality. *International Journal of Intercultural Relations, 29*(6), 651–673.

Index

M.B. Salzman, *A Psychology of Culture*, International and Cultural Psychology,
https://doi.org/10.1007/978-3-319-69420-7

FSC
www.fsc.org
MIX
Papier | Fördert
gute Waldnutzung
FSC® C003411

Kolibri 360 GmbH
Ferdinand-Jühlke-Straße 7
99095 Erfurt, Deutschland
produktsicherheit@kolibri360.de